KV-060-638

The
Bottle-Collector's
Guide

The
Bottle-Collector's
Guide

Geoffrey Wills

Drawings by Roger D. Penhallurick

BUCKS COUNTY LIBRARY

T, | A & B | 30/79T

R
74 8.8
WIL

John Bartholomew & Son Limited
Edinburgh and London

First published in Great Britain 1977 by
JOHN BARTHOLOMEW & SON LIMITED
12 Duncan Street, Edinburgh EH9 1TA
And 216 High Street, Bromley BR1 1PW

© Geoffrey Wills, 1977
All rights reserved. No part of this publication may be reproduced,
stored in a retrieval system, or transmitted, in any form, or by any
means, electronic, mechanical, photocopying, recording, or otherwise, without the prior permission of John Bartholomew & Son
Limited.

ISBN 0 7028 1007 X

Line drawings © Roger Penhallurick and John Bartholomew & Son
Limited

Phototypeset in V.I.P. Bembo by
Western Printing Services Ltd, Bristol

Printed in Great Britain

Contents

Acknowledgements

The writer is grateful to friends and correspondents in all parts of the world who have answered queries, and put forward more of their own; to others who have discussed, verbally or by letter, many aspects of a shared interest, and assisted in illuminating dark corners of the subject; and to others again who have helped in providing illustrations. In particular:

Robert J. Charleston President of the Glass Collectors' Circle, London, and formerly Curator, Department of Ceramics, Victoria & Albert Museum

Peter Cook Consultant Editor, *Australasian Antique Collector,* N.S.W., Australia

H. L. Douch Curator, The County Museum, Truro, Cornwall

Margaret Ellison Newcastle upon Tyne

Benno M. Forman Research Fellow, H. F. du Pont Winterthur Museum, Winterthur, Delaware, U.S.A.

Ivor Noël Hume Chief Archaeologist, Colonial Williamsburg, Va., U.S.A.

Olive Jones Material Culture Research (Glass), National Historic Parks & Sites, Ottawa, Canada

Alan Lupton Johannesburg, South Africa

Barry Taylor Managing Director, Wheaton Historical Association, Millville, N.J., U.S.A.

Alan Tomlin Ermington, Devon

John Wade Curator, Department of Applied Arts, Museum of Applied Arts & Sciences, Sydney, N.S.W., Australia

Not least, my thanks are due to Roger Penhallurick for taking infinite pains over the many drawings.

G.W.

Foreword

The present volume owes its inception to the exhibition of glass bottles held in the summer of 1976 at the County Museum, Truro, Cornwall. It was an assemblage of more than 200 pre-1850 wine bottles and seals, together with comparable arrays of mineral-water and other bottles. The gathering of so many examples in a single gallery provided an unrivalled opportunity to examine and compare them, and to make many re-assessments. The results of handling so many bottles of all kinds, with the addition of documentary material only recently made public in a limited form, have been incorporated in these pages. Much fresh information is printed for the first time, and more appears for the first time in book form.

Interest in old bottles was first shown in those used for wine; both their 'quaint' shapes and the fact that many of them bore dates aroused the interest of a few collectors. They received a brief footnote mention in Albert Hartshorne's pioneer work, *Old English Glasses* (1897), where he stated that he owned a specimen sealed 'WINGERWORTH 1711'. More considered treatment was given to the subject by a well-known glass-collector, Rees Price, in 1908. In that year he published 'Notes on the Evolution of the Wine-bottle' in the *Transactions of the Glasgow Archaelogical Society*. After a further interval, E. T. Leeds, of the Ashmolean Museum, wrote in *The Antiquary,* in 1914, an article entitled 'On the Dating of Glass Wine-bottles of the Stuart Period'. The same writer dealt at length with his home ground in '17th and 18th Century Wine-Bottles of Oxford Taverns' in *Oxoniensia* in 1941. The same facet of the subject was further explored and enlarged in that journal by Jeremy Haslam in 1969 and 1970

W. A. Thorpe contributed to the general study, and the formation in 1937 of the Circle of Glass Collectors brought together collectors and experts. The information available up to 1949 was summarized and considerably augmented by Lady Sheelah Ruggles-Brise in her book *Sealed Bottles*. She had made use of the correspondence columns of *Country Life* and the *Sunday Times* to elicit information from readers, and had communicated with the directors and curators of museums throughout the British Isles. As the Second World War had terminated only a few years previously, her task was no easy one and her success the greater under the conditions then prevailing.

Since that time a completely new variety of bottle-collecting has emerged: the acquisition of mineral-water bottles, beer bottles, pharmacy bottles, and, by and large, any bottles whatsoever. Such bottles are recovered from rubbish-dumps, river-beds, and hedges, and there is an international network of collectors' clubs and magazines to organize the hobby. Numerous books and articles dealing with these comparatively modern bottles, which are mainly of Victorian or later date, have been published in England, America, and elsewhere. Understandably, Americans have shown a particular interest in the bottles made in their land, from spirit flasks to 'hobble skirts', and all have been researched and listed.

The Making of Glass Bottles

Glass bottles are nowadays looked upon as commonplace expendables, and are largely taken for granted; it is quicker, and sometimes safer, to throw them away when emptied than to clean and re-use them. Whether the bottles are strictly utilitarian or not, an appreciation of them can be enriched by an understanding of their manufacture. While processes have been improved, the basic ingredients of glass, silica, and an alkali remain unaltered. It never ceases to amaze that such simple and unpromising ingredients can be transformed by heat into functional articles like bottles, as well as into ornamental objects of outstanding beauty.

In practice, the silica can be sand or certain kinds of stones, and the alkali might take the alternative forms of potash or soda. Pure silica requires great heat to melt it, but the presence of an alkali acts as a flux in making it flow at a more manageable temperature. Small amounts of other substances are added to the silica and alkali when it is required to improve the finished product. For example, it was duly found that the green tint present in so much old glass, caused by impurities in sand and stones, could be neutralized by the addition of a small amount of oxide of manganese in the mixture of ingredients: the 'batch'. The batch in its fused state is known to glassmakers as the 'metal', a term often applied also to the material of which the finished article is composed. Thus, wine bottles may be described as being of green or brown metal; the colours of the impure glass of which they were normally made. In the eighteenth century both green and brown bottles were sometimes classed together and described confusingly as 'black', a term that has been revived for them in modern times.

The earliest bottle-like hollow glass vessels were produced in ancient Egypt from about the sixteenth century B.C. Surviving specimens seldom measure more than 12 or 15cm. in height, their size being restricted by the process used in making them. This process involved taking a metal rod on which a lump of clay was shaped to the interior of the proposed vessel. On this was spread a paste of powdered glass and adhesive, and the whole was then heated until the glass melted. When cool, the rod was removed and the clay core chipped away. Later, a similar clay shape was wound with a thread of semi-molten glass, or with several differently coloured threads, then re-heated and rolled to fuse the strands. When cool it was treated in the same manner as in the earlier method. Surviving examples provide evidence of how they were made, because many still retain inside them fragments of the core.

An important advance in technique occurred in about the first century B.C. when it was discovered that molten glass on the end of a tube could be inflated in the same manner as a soap bubble. It meant that the dimensions of a hollow vessel were limited only by the strength of the blower's lungs and his ability in handling the blowing-tube. Not only were bottles thus free-blown, that is to say, of simple globular or ovoid shape, but they could also be blown into moulds. The moulds could be shaped, ornamented, or even inscribed, within limits, so that any marking on their interiors would appear on the surfaces of the finished articles.

Excavated bottles that had been made during the period of the Roman Empire, from about 100 B.C. onwards, exhibit a great variety of shapes and sizes, although the larger ones are scarce because of their susceptibility to damage. The majority are in a thinly-blown pale-green metal, and a large proportion are to some degree iridescent.

Buried glass is liable to attack by acid in the soil, which causes the structure to become laminated and attain an attractive multi-coloured appearance (see Plates 27 and 39). Immersion in water results in a filling of the cracks and layers so that the iridescence disappears, but it returns after the article has dried. It should be mentioned that an object with such a surface should be handled carefully, as the laminations are liable to flake off.

Once the technique of glass-blowing was known, a successful method of bottle-making evolved, one that remained little altered until the nineteenth century, when machinery displaced the craftsman for the purpose. The process was the same whether employed by a small group of men working in a primitive manner in a forest, or by the skilled staff of a well-organized brick-built glasshouse.

In brief and in general, the first requirement was to assemble the ingredients in correct quantities, mixing them thoroughly to form the batch. Each maker doubtless relied on his own well-tried recipe, but despite local variations the end-products differed little from one another. In 1758 Robert Dossie, who wrote of the manufactures current in his day, printed some recipes for making bottle glass. Among them, the simplest was:

> Take of wood-ashes two hundred pounds, and of sand one hundred pounds. Mix them thoroughly well by grinding them.

Dossie mentioned that the scoria or clinkers from an iron furnace 'may be added with great advantage', and suggested the use of 50lb. of scoria with 170lb. of ashes and 100lb. of sand.

Nearly a century later Andrew Ure printed some further recipes in which the ingredients were more varied than those given by Dossie. Ure, whose book was published in 1853, included the ashes of seaweed, glauber salts, and what were called 'soaper salts': an alkaline by-product of soap manufacture. He also listed broken glass or 'cullet', which could form as much as 25 per cent of a batch.

Cullet assisted in the melting by enabling it to take place at a lower temperature, was an economy, and had for a long time been recognized as an important ingredient of glass-making. Late in the seventeenth century it was noted that 'Many hundreds of poor families keep themselves from the Parish by picking up broken glass of all sorts to sell to the Maker', and all waste within a glasshouse was invariably retained for re-use. This fact explains the dearth of fragments at the sites of old glasshouses, in distinct contrast to the quantities of shards normally found where a pottery existed.

After mixing, the batch was shovelled into a large fire-clay crucible or 'pot', usually one of several standing in the furnace. The pots were each placed before an opening in the side of the furnace through which access could be gained to the melted glass, and there were other openings at which the craftsmen could re-heat their work during manufacture.

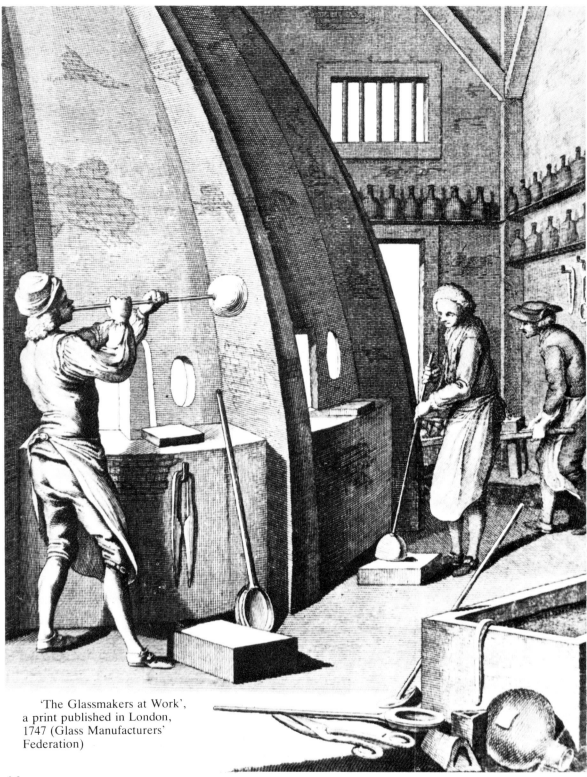

'The Glassmakers at Work',
a print published in London,
1747 (Glass Manufacturers'
Federation)

16

1   Pharmacy bottles lettered (left) J R BURDSALL'S ARNICA LINIMENT NEW YORK, and (right) HUNT'S LINIMENT PREPARED BY C E STANTON SING SING N.Y. American, mid-19th century, heights 14.6 and 11.4cm.

2   Veterinary bottles, and a surgeon's bottle (second from right) sealed JEWEL. Heights 20.2cm., 18.1cm., 16cm. and 19.3cm.

3 Pharmacy bottles lettered (left) FENNER'S KIDNEY & BACKACHE CURE, and (right) WARNER'S DIABETES CURE. American, *c.* 1880–90, heights 26 and 24.1cm.

4 Roman handled bottles, that on the left moulded on the base FRONTIN O. Heights 18.1cm., 22cm. and 12.9cm.

5   Pharmacy bottles: (left) lettered
SCHENCK'S PULMONIC SYRUP,

6   Mineral water bottles lettered (left)
MILLVILLE GLASS WORKS, and
(right) DYOTTVILLE GLASS
WORKS PHILAD ᴬ. American, *circa*
1870–80, heights 18.4cm.

7   Case bottles. 18th century, heights 29.8cm., 40cm., 23.2cm. and 31.5cm.

8   Lettered (left to right) WARNER'S SAFE TONIC BITTERS ROCHESTER N.Y.; DR J HOHSTETTER'S STOMACH BITTERS; BAKER'S ORANGE GROVE BITTER; and S.B. GOFF'S HERB BITTERS CAMDEN N.J. with printed label and carton. American, *circa* 1880–1900. Heights 19cm., 24.7cm., 23.8cm. and 13.6cm.

9   Wide-mouthed bottle for preserves,
excavated at York and showing iridescence. Late 17th/early 18th century,
height 15.2cm.

10   Oval-bodied bottles, sealed (left)
Thomas Glyn Owner, *c.* 1720, height
18.1cm., (right) WD 1725, height
18.1cm.

11 Unopened Codd bottle containing lemonade, lettered IRONS WADE-BRIDGE. Height 22.7cm. From Wade-bridge, Cornwall

12 Oil-can lettered INDE-PENDENCE BELL OILER 1876, issued to commemorate the centennial of the signing of the Declaration of Inde-pendence. American, height overall 12cm.

13 Sauce bottles. Heights 21cm. and 18.5cm.

14 Household and pharmacy bottles lettered (left to right) FELLOWS & Cº CHEMISTS Sᵀ JOHN N.B [Canada], FLORIDA WATER MURRAY & LANMAN DRUGGISTS NEW YORK, HATHAWAY'S PEERLESS GLOSS MADE IN U S A. Heights 15.5cm., 22.8cm. and 12.5cm.

15 Coloured, ribbed, shaped and lettered bottles for poison

16   Group of medicine-chest bottles

17   Chemist's shelf bottles, that on the right with a pourer and measure under the domed cover. Heights 18.5cm. and 22cm.

The majority of bottles were produced from the least expensive materials, resulting in the production of what is commonly termed 'bottle glass'. Best-quality ornamental and other articles were made of 'flint' or 'lead' glass; so named on account of its ingredients having included oxide of lead and, experimentally, ground flints. True lead or flint glass was occasionally used for small-sized bottles, and an imitation of it, colourless and misleadingly referred to as flint, was also employed. In both instances such bottles were for medicines and drugs.

All hollow articles, whether of the best or the poorest quality metal, have a common beginning, with the craftsman dipping the end of his blowing-iron into the pot. He removes it with a 'gather' of glass on it, roughly shapes it into a small cylinder (a 'paraison') on an iron slab or 'marver', and putting the tube to his mouth starts blowing. A sphere results, and from this a bottle-neck can be drawn by gentle swinging and manipulation. Alternatively, the gather is lowered into an open-topped wood or metal mould and blown therein, the neck being produced in a further operation.

The men in a glasshouse worked in a group or 'shop' of three or more, the foreman of each shop being known as the 'gaffer', his principal assistant being the 'servitor'. The servitor did the gathering and blowing, and then handed the iron with its breath-filled bubble to the gaffer seated in the 'chair': the latter being a bench-like seat with two arms and no back, the arms supporting the iron while the occupant of the chair worked on the article being made.

Neck finishes ranging in date from *c.* 1660.

C. 1660

Outline drawing of a bottle
showing the kick-up

C. 1670

1697

C. 1700

Rolling the iron to and fro along the chair-arms ensured that the semi-molten glass did not droop and that it retained a balanced shape. The base of the bottle was then pushed inwards to form a conical depression, known as the 'kick-up' or 'push-up'. The succeeding operation was for one of the shop to take a solid iron rod with a slightly broadened end, known as a 'pontil' or 'punty', and with a small gather on it bring it to the chair. With the aid of the gather the pontil was attached to the centre of the kick-up; the gather sometimes first being twirled in sand or dust to ensure that it did not adhere too strongly. The blowing-iron could then be removed, or 'cracked-off', by touching the neck of the bottle with a wetted stick or a piece of cold iron, and the part-completed article would be held on the pontil.

Alternatively, the blowing-iron that had already done service was employed in the manner of a pontil. The iron was cracked off the neck as the bottle rested in a cradle, then the fragments of glass remaining on the end of the blowing-iron were re-heated and the tool used as described above. This method, which was not uncommon in France, left a scar in the form of a rough-surfaced ring. A further variant procedure, current between about 1845–80, employed a bare pontil, which, when raised to a red heat, adhered adequately. It left a round smooth scar faced with iron oxide and red or black in colour.

At this stage the neck could be given its 'finish': a term used to describe shaping the neck rim, and in the instance of a wine bottle the addition of the string-rim. The latter, a narrow raised band encircling the top of the neck, was applied in the form of one or more threads of glass. Its justification was to provide an anchorage for string or wire used to hold a closure in place. Its other function, and a reason for its general retention, was to strengthen the neck where it was likely to be damaged; it provides a good reinforcement when a cork is forced into place. The finish, being executed by hand, varied in appearance, even if only slightly, and each craftsman left his individual 'mark'.

On completion of the finish, the bottle was broken away from the pontil by smartly tapping the latter, leaving a scar that varied in both size and appearance: the 'pontil mark'. The kick-up not only ensured that the bottle stood steadily, but kept the pontil mark clear of a table-top or any other surface that it might damage.

When a seal was added to a wine bottle it was applied by

dropping a blob of molten glass on the selected spot. This was quickly impressed with an engraved stamp. Generally it was done with a disc of brass or other metal, but in some instances pairs of initials were impressed from single letters mounted in a handle. This method was comparable to the setting of printing-type in a chase, and would seem to have been used only for a short time in the second half of the seventeenth century. To obtain a clear impression it was necessary for the disc or letters to be hot, and wood was unsuitable for the purpose. A Newcastle glassmaker tried it in 1812, but had to have the work executed again in metal.

Finally, the bottle required annealing: that is, cooling very slowly so as to cancel out the stresses set up in it during manufacture. For the purpose it was placed in the annealing chamber, 'arch' or 'leer', which might be in an area of the furnace where the temperature could be gradually lowered. After about 1780 the tunnel leer was in use, the long tunnel containing trays to hold the newly-made wares. Heat was concentrated at the start, and the trays were very slowly pushed or pulled along to the far end, where it was little warmer than the outside air.

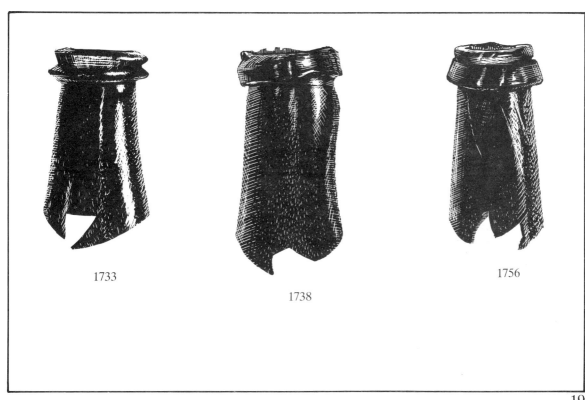

1733

1738

1756

1774

1784

1788

1790

C. 1800

1815

Forming a bottle by blowing into a mould had been practised in Roman times, resulting in an article of distinctive appearance and of uniform size and shape. For many centuries this applied only to the body of the container, and the lip still had to be finished by hand in a separate operation; a process taking time to perform and calling for the services of a skilled man. Nevertheless, speed was not lacking, doubtless because a shop was paid according to its output. It was noted that:

> This operation, which goes on continuously and regularly, occupies about half a minute. As soon as one workman has left a mould, another, with a similar lump of red-hot glass, takes his place; and so quickly is the whole process carried forward, that one workman can form the necks of the bottles which three others are employed in blowing.

Moulds were in use in England from at least early in the seventeenth century. Jeremy Haslam notes that a bottle in his possession 'is dateable to about 1730 [and] has a distinctive mark of a wide cylindrical mould on the body'. Bottles of octagonal section, which were in production by about the same time as the foregoing, could only have been made in moulds, and the same applied to the contemporaneous case bottles.

Important information on the use of moulds has been published by Margaret Ellison, and relates to the cutting of inscriptions on brass and iron moulds for the use of glass-makers at Newcastle, Gateshead, and South Shields. She has transcribed the surviving account books of the engraving workshop run by Ralph Beilby and Thomas Bewick between 1767 and 1797, and continued by Bewick or his son until 1848. Ralph Beilby was the brother of William, remembered for his delicate enamelling on glass, not infrequently of amorial bearings, and Thomas Bewick is no less renowned for his wood-engraving: a form of illustration by woodcuts that led to a revival of the then neglected art.

Bewick began his seven-year apprenticeship with Ralph Beilby in 1767 at the age of fourteen, entering a workshop where the output comprised 'pipe-moulds, bottle-moulds, brass clock-faces, coffin-plates, stamps, seals, bill-heads, crests, and ciphers'. At the end of his term he spent a short period in London, and then returned to Newcastle to enter into partnership with Beilby until the latter retired in 1797. From then until 1812 Bewick ran the

Seal cut at the Beilby and Bewick workshop, Newcastle. Diameter 3.5 cm. (Norfolk Museums Service)

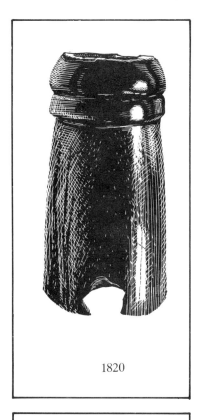

1820

1828

business on his own, from 1812 to 1825 was partnered by his son, Robert Elliot Bewick, and from 1825 to 1848 the latter had it to himself. Ralph Beilby died in 1817, Thomas Bewick in 1828, and his son in 1849.

The Beilby and Bewick workshop papers reveal a variety of information concerning bottle-moulding during the years they cover. The majority of the orders were for pharmaceutical containers, and it is to be noted that in some instances old and worn moulds were re-cut or repaired. Brass was the metal employed until 1819, when cast-iron first received a mention, and a pewter mould was tried in 1822. One entry relates to the engraving of a seal as part of a mould, 'presumably to produce a moulded bottle looking like the traditional sealed bottle'. This took place in 1815, and the result must have been the forerunner of the present-day practice, which saves cost and superficially resembles the real thing.

It must be borne in mind, however, that the workshop only handled moulds requiring the cutting of inscriptions in them; plain ones, like those for the bodies of wine bottles, would not have come their way. The numerous entries make it amply clear that by at least 1767 bottle-moulding was a normal practice at the several glasshouses in the Newcastle area, and there is no reason to suppose that it was not equally commonplace elsewhere. Some proof of this is gained from a news paragraph that appeared in *Felix Farley's Bristol Journal* of 15 August 1752:

> On Thursday James Watkins was committed to Newgate for stealing one Brass Bottle-mould, value 18s., the property of Mr. Thomas Warren & Co. from the Glasshouse in St. Thomas Street in this City. It seems the said Watkins worked at the glasshouse, and sold the mould to a Brazier of this City at a market price.

A month later, the *Journal* reported that Watkins had been acquitted of stealing *two* bottle moulds.

By 1822 a Bristol maker, Henry Ricketts, had devised and patented a mould in which were formed both the body and neck of the bottle. The patent, No. 4623, was for 'An Improvement in the Art or Method of Making or Manufacturing Glass Bottles, such as are Used for Wine, Porter, Beer, or Cyder'. Granted on 5 December 1821, it was enrolled on 26 January of the year following, and the inventor stated that it was an 'improvement upon the construction of all moulds heretofore used in the manufacture of bottles'.

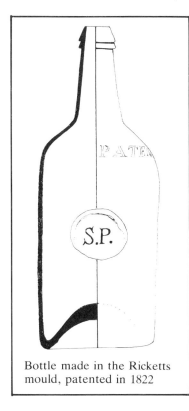

Bottle made in the Ricketts mould, patented in 1822

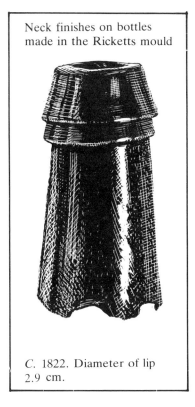

Neck finishes on bottles made in the Ricketts mould

C. 1822. Diameter of lip 2.9 cm.

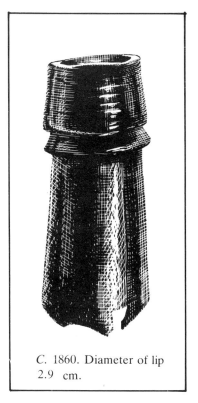

C. 1860. Diameter of lip 2.9 cm.

The heart of the apparatus was a hinged cast–iron mould that was normally kept open by gravity, so that the paraison could be introduced. Then, the operator stood on a pedal to close the mould, removing his foot from it when the bottle had been blown. The arrangement of pedals and levers permitted the use of any mould required, and it was easily adaptable to produce bottles of large or small capacities.

Thirty years later Andrew Ure described a similar mould in use. He wrote of the blower having marvered his gather into a paraison and introduced it into the open mould. Then, the narrative continues, he shuts the mould by pressing a pedal with his foot:

> and holding his tube vertically, blows through it, so as to expand the cooling glass into the form of the mould. Whenever he takes his foot from the pedal-lever, the mould spontaneously opens out into two halves, and falls asunder by its bottom hinge. He then lifts the bottle up at the end of the rod, and transfers it to the finisher, who, touching the glass-tube at the end of the pipe with a cold iron, cracks off the bottle smoothly at its mouth-ring. The finished bottles are immediately piled up in the hot annealing arch, where they are afterwards allowed to cool slowly for 24 hours at least.

Seal; the guide-lines used by the engraver can be seen. Diameter of impression 3.4 cm.

The foregoing description applied only to the manufacture of moulded bottles that were left with the neck-rim plain. The Ricketts and other moulds did not include the finish, so that a string-rim or any other shaping would have to be added in a separate operation. Some kind of tool would seem to have been used in conjunction with the Ricketts mould, because bottles made in it are invariably found to have the distinctive feature of a lip with a deep cone above a narrow one. Introduction of such an aid would have had the effect of further lessening reliance on the experienced eye and dexterous hand of the craftsman. Later, a tool was devised for forming the internal threads in the necks of screw-top bottles.

Until the first quarter of the nineteenth century the bottle-making industry had made only slight progress, but after this time the tempo quickened. The 123 bottle-houses recorded as being in operation in 1833 increased to 240 by 1874, and in the intervening years a number of firms that later achieved eminence were established. A noteworthy advance was made in 1860, when C. W. & F. Siemens patented their regenerative furnace; in it, gas was produced from coal in a separate operation, the gas being burned with air in the furnace proper. The gains were not only in a saving of fuel costs, but solid fuel and its smoke were kept away from the pots: impurities therefore did not contaminate the metal, as they were all too often prone to do under conventional conditions. Further improvements were made to the Siemens furnace, which was at first used for making sheet glass but within ten years of its introduction was being employed in bottle manufacture.

The 'snap', a spring-loaded grip, was introduced in the 1850s as a replacement for the pontil. The advantage of the snap was its simplicity, and an additional feature was that it left no mark. With its use the kick-up was only an anachronism as there was no pontil-mark to conceal.

Despite these and other advances there were many glasshouses that continued unchanged. In America there was a move towards a shop comprising seven men, of whom three were skilled and interchangeable in their rôles. It resulted in an increase in output of the order of 138 per cent over the traditional four-man shop. However, when attempts were made to introduce the American system to England they failed owing to the strength of union opposition.

On both sides of the Atlantic much thought was being

given to mechanization as a means of raising output as well as reducing the amount of skilled labour required. In America a simple type of bottle-making machine was patented in 1882. Four years later, in England, two men from Ferrybridge, Yorkshire, Howard Ashley, manager of an iron foundry, and Josiah Arnall, a postmaster, collaborated in patenting a practical machine requiring a minimum of trained manpower to operate it. The Ashley bottlemaker operated in reverse of the normal method: it formed the finish first and then the body, using compressed air for blowing. It required a skilled man to feed it with gathers of glass, but with the aid of six labourers he could produce 144 bottles an hour. The machine was revolutionary, and led the way to bigger and increasingly efficient inventions.

These were developed and built in the United States and then throughout the world. By 1903 it had been found possible to gather the glass by means of an arm sucking it from the pot or tank of molten metal to feed the mould. As an alternative a gravity-fed machine was developed: a paddle pushed a pre-determined amount of molten glass over the edge of the tank, where it was sheared off and blown to shape in a mould.

Traces of the use of moulds can usually be seen on the finished products; this applies whether the mould is filled by a man with a blowing-iron or by a machine using compressed air. For example, a simple mould for forming the body occasionally leaves a horizontal ridge where its open top ended, and a two-part mould hinging at the base leaves a line running across the base and up each side. Bottles made in a Ricketts mould have a noticeable raised line encircling the top of the body and one up each side of the shoulder. Many bottles originating in France and elsewhere on the mainland of Europe were rotated in their moulds during blowing. This smoothed any seams, but often replaced them with distinctive horizontal marks encircling the body.

French sealed wine bottle
labelled Vieux Cognac 1811.
Circa 1860, height 33.3 cm.
(Alan Tomlin)

Seal on bottle
depicting the comet of 1811.
Diameter 4 cm.

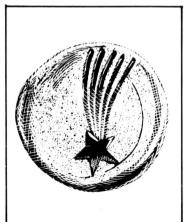

Bottle-making in Europe, America, and British Colonies

Most of the bottles used in the British Isles in early times were imported: the small industry set up under the Romans could supply only a portion of the country's needs. At the time, there were bigger undertakings active on the mainland of Europe, at Cologne and in Northern France. Amiens, for example, was almost certainly the site, in the third–fourth centuries A.D., of a glasshouse owned by a man named Frontinus, who put his name on some of his blown and moulded wares. Some were lettered 'FRONTIN O,' and comparable pieces are recorded inscribed with the name Daccius (Plate 4).

Positive evidence of further local manufacture does not occur until the thirteenth century, at which date itinerant glassmakers emigrated from across the Channel. They settled at first in the well-wooded areas of the south coast, where there were good supplies of sand and timber, the latter serving not only for fuel, but as a source of potash, which was a constituent of its ashes. Likewise, bracken grew plentifully and could be burned for employment in a similar manner. By the succeeding century some of these glassmakers from Normandy had established themselves in parts of Kent, Surrey, and Sussex, where subsequent excavations have revealed that they made small vessels, including bottles. Their output was described at the time as comprising 'urinals [for medical use], bottles, bowls, cups to drink and such like', of which fragments in a coarse green-tinted metal have been found.

It was not until the end of the sixteenth century that a more stable industry came into being. The Venetians had gained an almost complete monopoly in glass-making, their products being exported throughout Europe and their craftsmen being strictly forbidden to leave their native land. Nevertheless, many of the more adventurous workers braved the threatened dire punishments by seeking their fortunes further afield. Settling here and there, they helped to build glasshouses and taught their skills to the local employees.

After an initial failure in 1549, a further group of foreign workers settled in London in 1570, and from then onwards the industry slowly prospered. In 1614, Sir Robert Mansell, then Treasurer of the Navy and later vice-Admiral of England, began to take an interest in glassmaking. Nine years later he was granted a monopoly in glassmaking throughout the country, his patent permitting him to manufacture wares of all kinds. The specification, dated 22 May 1623, stated that he was empowered to carry out

> melting and makeing of all manner of drinking glasses, broade glasses, window glasses, looking glasses, and all other kinde of glasse, glasses, bugles-[beads], bottles, violls [phials], or vessels whatsoever made of glasse . . . with seacoals, pittcoale, or any other fewell whatsoever not being tymber or wood.

The condition that only coal ('seacoale' transported by coaster, or 'pittcoale' overland from the pithead) should be employed in the furnaces was in accord with Government policy. Ever since the days of the Spanish Armada there had been concern over the dwindling supplies of home-grown timber for ship-building. The principal other users were iron-founders and makers of glass, and James I made determined efforts to prohibit both of these industries from having access to what had been their traditional and plentiful fuel. In both instances it was no simple matter to make a change, and processes had to be adjusted to meet the circumstances.

In glassmaking, as Eleanor Godfrey makes clear, the change took place in the construction of furnaces, and success was attained by burning the coal over a grate to which was led a draught from outside the building. In addition, a chimney at the top not only took away smoke and fumes, but increased the draught. Much higher temperatures could be reached, and in due course it was possible to melt, blow, and manipulate the metal to produce the distinctive English wine bottle.

Bottles were part of the output of makers of what was termed 'green glass': metal used for making other than colourless Venetian-type articles, and window glass. Much of it had always been made by small groups of workers moving from place to place as supplies of wood gave out. With the switch to coal and Mansell's reorganization of the entire industry, the itinerants gave way to larger units near coalfields, sand beds, and clay, the latter for making the pots.

Around 1600 bottles, other than phials, were mostly imported. They were thin-walled, pale in colour, requiring a wicker or leather covering for protection, or were supplied in sets in compartmented boxes. They came mainly from France, but demand for them was not heavy as the use of bottles had not yet become widespread.

The makers of green glass in England were mostly of foreign origin, kept their secrets in their families and proved difficult to control even by an admiral. In 1639 Mansell reported to the House of Lords on his achievements to date, mentioning, in addition to much else concerning glass,

> Green-Glasses – Of all sorts are made likewise of English Materialls, which works after I had sustained great losse, and undergone great vexation (in the disposing of them) I let to a gentleman of known honesty, and of experience in Glasse.

The latter remains anonymous and equally unknown is the date of the transaction, but whoever he was he would appear to have been among the first men responsible for producing a new kind of bottle: the English wine bottle. A striking contrast to those hitherto available, being strong, thick-walled, and dark in colour. Its making involved particular skills and different metal, so in due course bottle-making became a separate branch of the glass industry.

It was at the end of the century that John Houghton, a writer, published a list of glasshouses in his book *Letters for the Improvement of Trade and Husbandry*. The relevant 'letter' was dated 15 May 1696, and gave the number of active establishments in England and Wales, stating whether they made flint or sheet glass or bottles. Of the bottle manufactories Houghton recorded the following:

In and about London and Southwark	9
Topsham, near Exeter	1
Oddam, near Bath, and Chellwood, Somerset	3
In and about Bristol	6
Gloucester ⎫ Glos.	3
Newnham ⎭	2
Swansea	1
Oakengates, Shropshire	1
Stourbridge, Worcs.	5
Nottingham ⎫	1
Awsworth ⎬ Notts.	1
Custom-more, near Awsworth ⎭	1
Near Silkstone ⎫ Yorkshire	1
Near Ferrybridge ⎭	1
Kings Lynn ⎫ Norfolk	1
Yarmouth ⎭	1
Newcastle upon Tyne	4

The locations of the 42 glasshouses show that the industry was widespread, and its success was underlined by Houghton who said that so far as he knew only eight dozen bottles had been imported into the country during the whole of 1696. In that same year it was recorded that the annual output in England amounted to some 240,000 dozen bottles: not far short of three million.

A feature of the history of English glass-making was the intermittent restriction suffered by the industry through Government policy. Under Oliver Cromwell a tax was levied on all glass wares at the rate of one shilling in the pound sterling. Then, some decades later, in 1695, William III called for a heavier contribution towards the expense of the current war against the French. On this occasion, flint or best-quality glass was charged at the rate of 20 per cent of its value and bottles a shilling a dozen. The Act of Parliament authorizing the levy made it valid for a period of five years, but a year later it was revised and the levy made permanent.

The glass industry rose as one man, and every possible argument was advanced against the imposition. In the event, contrary to normal Government reaction to such lamentations, the tax was halved. More to the point, in mid 1699 it was completely abolished and the glassmakers were left in peace.

Their freedom lasted for almost half a century until in 1745 the Government tried again, and with greater success. On this occasion, while the divergences in the rates remained, the duty was levied in a different manner. Instead of an overall percentage or a charge on the value of the finished articles, the maker paid on the weight of raw materials used. This was at the rate of 2s. 4d. on bottle glass and 9s. 4d. on better quality metal, in each instance the amount being payable on every 112lb.

Following earlier rises, the duty was again raised in 1777 and at the same time the categories were slightly altered. Bottle glass was to be charged at 3s. 6d. per 112lb., and the higher rate was thenceforward to be paid on 'Phial Glass', which was bracketed with best quality flint at 18s. 8d. per 112lb.

By 1812 the duty had reached such a high level that the national output of the industry began to fall, and in the period 1812–15 a decrease of more than 35 per cent was recorded in comparison with the preceding three years. Not only did the burden of taxation inhibit production, but the stringent regulations and the methods of collection were grievous burdens. It was enacted in the reign of William IV that the duty should be charged

> on the gross Gauge of such Materials or Metal or other Pre-parations in the Pot, of which fluxed Materials. . . . Three thousand two hundred being taken as the Specific Gravity, Eleven·shall be the Circular Divisor for finding the Contents in each Pot in Pounds Weight Avoirdupois.

Alternatively, duty was levied on the weight of finished products as they came from the leer. This was recollected by A. C. Powell, a Bristol bottle manufacturer, who wrote in 1925:

> The annealing arches were placed under the seal of the Excise Officers and I remember seeing the projecting bars upon which the scales used to be hung to weigh the bottles (of course in their presence) as they were 'drawn'. The cost of extra handling and the inevitable breakage must have added considerably to the cost of manufacture, not to mention the delay in suiting the con-venience of the representatives of the Crown. In some cases the glass was weighed over a second time! Altogether this method of obtaining revenue must have been what in these days would be called 'unscientific', for it was a direct hindrance to trade.

An inevitable effect of the high rate of duty was the establishment of tax-dodging furnaces. Small, illicit glass-houses were set up in out-of-the-way places, and pro-liferated as the years passed; as the duties rose, so it became increasingly profitable to evade them. These shady con-cerns, known as 'cribs' or 'little-goes', made wares that could be sold cheaply, relying on plenty of cullet for quick melting and low costs. It was said that the operators used pots of small size, so that if they had the misfortune to be caught by the Excise men their liability for duty would not be too great.

Eventually, a Commission of Inquiry into the Excise examined makers and others, and in 1835 published its report on the situation. One of the glassmakers who gave evidence was Charles Mulvany, of Dublin. In an outburst that made up in honesty what it lacked in tact, Mulvany, a manufacturer of flint glass, spoke equally for his bottle-making brethren:

> By the existing state of the Excise laws, our business and premises are placed under the arbitrary control of a class of men, to whose authority and to whose caprice it is most irksome to have to submit, and this under a system of regulations most ungraciously inquisitorial. We cannot enter parts of our own premises without their permission; we can do no one single act in the conduct of our own business without having previously notified our intention to the officers placed over us. We have in the course of one week's operations to serve some sixty or seventy notices on these our masters, and this, too, under heavy penalties of from two to five hundred pounds for every separate neglect.

It is little wonder that after the Government finally abolished the duty in 1845, when bottle glass was paying 7s. per 112lb., the industry at last began to expand. The owners, managers, and workers had had to suffer for decades not only the crippling restraint of the continual presence of Customs men, but the system of taxation had effectively stifled experiment and progress. Duty being levied on the contents of the pot meant that any waste metal was charged at the same rate as the usable. Accidentally broken bottles were included in the tally when bottles were charged by weight. Under such circumstances trials to improve quality and output became too costly to be worth attempting.

Little information is available concerning the bottle-making industry compared with what is known about other types of glass manufacture. The main centres and the names of many of those who successfully, or unsuccessfully, owned and managed concerns are recorded, but details are usually lacking. The utilitarian bottle has, understandably, never attracted the attention of historians in the way that, say, cut-glass has done. Many of the records have vanished long ago, but in a few instances the story has been pieced together.

A case in point is the Alloa glassworks, in Scotland. It was founded on the initiative of Lady Frances Erskine, whose ancestors had founded the port of Alloa, on the Firth of Forth, where there were supplies of salt, sand, and seaweed, as well as coal from the family collieries. The opening of the glassworks in 1750 was probably what stirred the long-established concern at Leith, also beside the Firth, to draw attention to its existence. The *Gentleman's Magazine* noted in 1751:

> Leith, Scotland, Jan. 11. A globular bottle has been blown here capable of holding two hogsheads; the biggest ever produced at any glass-works, its dimensions 40 inches by 42.

Bottles formed an important part of the Alloa output. In 1767 the works came into the ownership of a company and eventually, like other establishments in England, some of its partners provided links with other glasshouses; 'Unity is Strength' was an unwritten motto of the industry. At Alloa the Geddes family had interests in glassmaking at Glasgow and Warrington as well as at Leith. With the expansion of the whisky trade in the nineteenth century a further outlet of increasing importance was to hand.

It was at Alloa that the first American-designed Owens machine to be operated in Britain was installed in about 1908.

Bottles made at Alloa from 1750 onwards do not differ in appearance from those made elsewhere. There seems to be no evidence that sealed examples were made, and the recorded sealed bottles bearing recognizably Scottish inscriptions could as well have been made by any of the other north-of-the-Border glasshouses. Equally, they could have been imported from England.

Mainland Europe

Broadly speaking, little research has been devoted to bottles and their manufacture in mainland Europe. Such everyday domestic articles have not been collected as avidly as elsewhere, and their study has consequently lacked a stimulus. Small containers for pharmaceutical purposes varied little, if at all, wherever they were produced, but wine bottles showed regional characteristics.

A centre of production in the Netherlands was Liége, where members of the Colinet (or Colnet) and Bonhomme families had interests in more than one establishment. It was, incidentally, a John Colinet who was involved closely in the initiation of wine-bottle manufacture in England, and there is no doubt that he was related to the men of the same name at Liége.

Raymond Chambon prints two nineteenth-century references to early bottles in the papers of a glassmaker named Amand Colinet. The entries are dated 1571–2 and 1604, and record orders for bottles to be supplied with a *'place pour mettre cire'*: a ring in relief on the shoulder within which a wax seal could be impressed. This might well have been the origin of such seals being made at later dates in glass, but ring-marked bottles of the kind have not survived and the question of their having existed is open to dispute.

Chambon also quotes a seal inscribed *'Indocus Goethals'* and bearing the date '1650'. It was recorded as being on a bottle belonging to Louis Minard-van Hoorebecke, a catalogue of whose collection of antiquities and curiosities was published at Ghent in 1886.

Likewise, in France there is evidence of early activity, but as elsewhere records are all too few. Sixteenth-century references include the mention of six and a half dozen glass bottles used at a banquet in Paris attended by Catherine de' Medici; Catherine married the future king, Henri II, in 1533, when she was fourteen years of age, and died in 1589.

During the same period various sizes of bottles were mentioned as being in use. They included the *pinte* and *chopine*, the latter having a capacity of half a *pinte*, the *pinte* measuring just short of a litre.

A wood-carving on a staircase in the Hôtel Jean Lallement, at Bourges in central France, dates from the first half of the sixteenth century and is illustrated by James Barrelet. The carving depicts a man brandishing a bottle that has a flat-based body and tall neck. The same writer also shows a green glass bottle of comparable shape, 27cm. in height, found at a depth of 4m. in the ruins of the Abbey of Saint-Basle, Champagne. The bottle bears a circular seal inscribed *'Sigillum monasterii sancti Balali'*, and is in the possession of M. Barrelet. He suggests that it may have been made at a glassworks at Argonne, in the north-east of the country, and dates it to the sixteenth century.

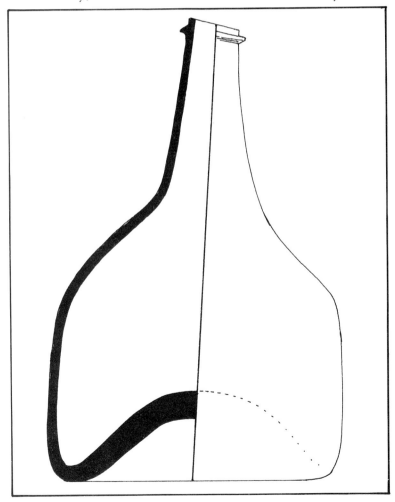

Dutch bottle, *c.* 1735.
Height 19.7 cm.

Bottles made in the Netherlands and France differed in both appearance and metal from their English counterparts. Netherlands examples made in the seventeenth century have oval bodies, followed later by spherical bodies and a somewhat shorter neck than formerly. The squat onion shape popular in England from about 1670 did not attain widespread use across the Channel until the turn of the century, and it was still in production after English makers had turned their attention to cylindrically-bodied containers. To sum up, the Netherlands bottles were usually being made at later dates than similar English ones, and in addition tended to have comparatively tall necks. Frequently, the top of the neck has a double ring of glass to form a 'W'-section string-rim, and the metal was at first green and later often amber in colour.

On the other hand, French eighteenth-century bottles favoured what is termed, appropriately, a 'flower-pot' shape, with the lower part of the body tapering towards the base. Alternatively, the bottles were of flattened oval form with a long neck, of brown glass covered in woven rushes or wicker.

It was perhaps to this second type that the first Earl of Bristol referred when he recorded payments on several occasions for flasks of French wines. Thus, on 29 September 1710 he paid Messrs. Bonet & Bennet £25 'for 100 Flasks of french Clarett'. Earlier, he had been buying such wine by the hogshead: for example, in 1706 he paid the same firm £43 'for one hogshead of Margous claret-wine'.

The metal used for French bottles did not always prove as durable as the English, and in many instances deteriorated in time. Not only did any rush or wicker casing rot away, but Ivor Noël Hume reports excavated examples that had changed in colour to black and that decayed 'rapidly to a sugarlike consistency'.

As the eighteenth century progressed the French bottle-making industry expanded and prospered. In 1800 there were 53 bottle houses, and by 1829 their output was 50 per cent of the total product of the entire glass industry. Mechanization began to make an appearance in the nineteenth century, by which date the shapes of bottles were becoming more or less standardized. Each wine-growing region favoured a particular style for its products: Burgundy was put into bottles with gently sloping shoulders, and Claret reached the market in bottles with rounded shoulders and short necks. Champagne required

German (Schleswig-Holstein) seals

1669

C. 1680

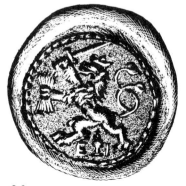

36

a bottle with thick walls, so that it had the strength to withstand the pressure of the gaseous contents.

The most familiar German bottle is the one always used for Hock, with its shoulderless and narrow profile, made in a pale-green or amber metal. In the past, sealed bottles enjoyed a degree of popularity and examples have survived. An instance is one of 1739 from the north of the country. In shape it is reminiscent of the French 'flower pot', but with incurving sides, a pronounced shoulder and a tall neck.

Italian wine was sold in a locally-made pear-shaped bottle encased in woven straw like some of the French examples, but with the addition of a woven foot so that it could stand upright. Such a bottle was known in eighteenth-century England as a Betty or Florence Flask. In 1736 Henry Purefoy wrote to London from his home in Buckinghamshire to inquire about 'a chest of fflorence wine in Betties'.

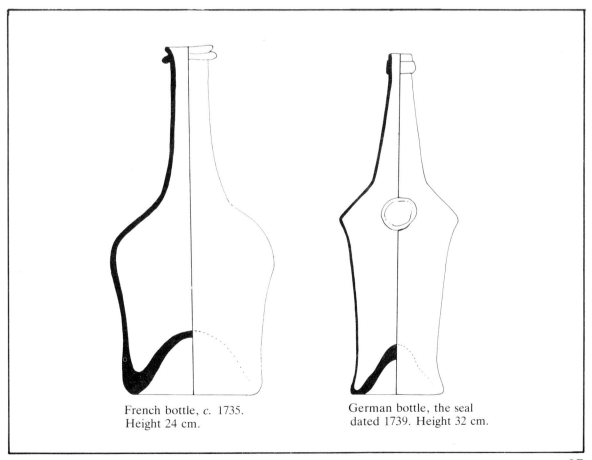

French bottle, c. 1735.
Height 24 cm.

German bottle, the seal dated 1739. Height 32 cm.

Colonial America and the United States

The early settlers at Jamestown, Virginia, are known to have made glass; in 1608, in the words of their leader, Captain John Smith: 'We sent home ample proof of Pitch, Tarre, Glasse'. The site of the glasshouse has been investigated, but although pieces of glass were found they were too small in size to yield information on what was made. This and a succeeding effort in 1621 ended in failure, and the colonists and their descendants had to rely on imported glass for many decades. That they did so is amply proved by the number of English-made bottles excavated, mostly in the form of fragments, from settlement sites. At Jamestown no fewer than 20,000 fragments have been recovered, some of which have been pieced together, and three bottles were excavated intact.

Among the fragments were 104 seals, some of them duplicates, of which several have been traced to their original owners. In a few instances the seals are those of English innkeepers, and another is that of The King's Bagnio, a London bathing-house. This bathing-house was one of several in the city, where visitors could bathe in medicinal waters from a spring. According to an account written in 1683, 'adjoining to the bagnio there are four little round rooms, about eight feet over, which are made for degrees of heat, some being hotter, others colder, as persons can best bear and are pleased to use'. The King's was situated in Long Acre, where it was first named after the Duke of York as The Duke's Bagnio; in 1686, after the Duke had become James II, the establishment was accordingly re-named. The seal certainly came from there, but it is not known how it reached Jamestown.

Similarly, the site of Williamsburg, also in Virginia, the state capital founded in 1632 and destroyed by fire 200 years later, has been painstakingly explored. Excavations have revealed impressive quantities of bottles and fragments that tell a story like that at Jamestown. As at the latter place, some of the seals show the names or initials of local inhabitants who ordered the bottles from England. At that time, and for a while later, the home government gave little or no encouragement to colonial manufacturers, and the inhabitants were expected to assist the British export trade rather than help themselves. Nevertheless, bottle-making did take place sporadically in America, but it proved to be no real threat to the livelihood of workers in Bristol and elsewhere in the homeland.

The first names of importance in American glassmaking are those of Caspar Wistar and his son, Richard. Caspar emigrated from Germany in 1717, opened a button-making factory at Philadelphia and in 1739 extended his interests to New Jersey. There, on a site duly named Wistarberg, he established a glasshouse. The elder man died in 1752 and both concerns were continued by the son, who advertised soon afterwards that he supplied window glass and 'most Sorts of Bottles, Gallon, Half Gallon, and Quart', as well as 'Half Gallon Case Bottles'. In 1780, following the War of Independence, with its social and economic consequences, and the death of Richard Wistar, the glasshouse was closed and the property sold.

During the same period another glasshouse was started at Manheim, some 70 miles from Philadelphia, by Henry William Stiegel. He, too, was a German, reaching America in 1750 when twenty-one years of age. He duly entered into partnership in an iron foundry, and after a number of short-lived glass-making projects erected his principal Manheim furnace. This was begun in 1768 and manufacturing followed two years later, but came to a halt in 1774 with Stiegel suffering a term of imprisonment for debt. As at Wistarberg, window glass and bottles were the staple output, the latter including half-gallons, quarts and pints (these sold at 12s., 6s., and 4s. 6d. per dozen, respectively).

A third, also short-lived, concern deserves a mention: that of the Glass House Company, New York. In 1754 it advertised for sale 'all sorts of Bottles from 1 Quart to 3 Gallons and upwards . . . and all Gentlemen that wants Bottles of any size with their Names on them . . . may . . .

Three seals excavated on the site of Williamsburg, Va. John Custis, alderman, 1678-1729; William Prentis, died 1765; John Greenhow, merchant, 1724-87

39

Seal of Ralph Wormley of Williamsburg, died ? 1651. It is composed of separate letters held together for impressing. Width *c.* 3 cm.

have them made with all Expedition'. It would appear that the business closed in 1768, because its founder, Matthew Earnest (or Ernest), was bankrupt.

Following the Declaration of Independence in 1776 the new United States slowly began to organize the production of goods that had hitherto come from across the ocean. Glass was high on the list, and by 1820 there were a number of active concerns catering for all needs. From that period onwards glassware was designed to suit the taste and requirements of the buyer, who had no longer to be satisfied with what European makers considered suitable. An American style in glassware, not least in bottles, became discernible. Among the new developments was the so-called 'chestnut' bottle or flask, with a globular flat-sided body and a resemblance in shape to the chestnut. The name is given to some without ornamentation and to others with relief patterns on the sides. Equally a speciality was the flat-sided flask, which had been produced in small quantities earlier, but really came into its own after about 1810. Usually of pocketable size, the flask held a handy drink of whisky or other spirit, the taking of which was customary, no doubt to alleviate the rough conditions of daily life. The hinged mould, which began to be employed for making flasks after 1810, resulted in an attractively-patterned vessel relatively cheap to produce and quickly catching the public's fancy. A minimum of skilled labour was involved in its production, as the neck was merely sheared and smoothed without the addition of a string-rim or other refinement (Plate 26).

The enterprise shown by the designers and makers of the flasks was directed also to other glass containers. Bottles for all kinds of liquids were produced in great numbers, most of them being skilfully shaped and coloured to catch the buyer's eye. The knell of many of these fancy articles was sounded finally by the automatic bottle-making machine, which wasted little time on ornament but produced plain functional containers by the million. It was the invention of Michael J. Owens, who worked as a blower with the Toledo Glass Company, Toledo, Ohio, established by E. D. Libbey in 1888. Owens's employer encouraged his experiments, which resulted in 1903 in the building of a machine weighing ten tons that did what was required of it. Within a few years he had developed this monster into one that was even bigger, and was capable of producing 625 gross (90,000) one-pint beer bottles in 24 hours: a far cry from the individually-blown hand-sealed examples of 250 years earlier.

British Colonies

For a long time the countries of the British Empire relied almost exclusively on glassware imported from England, together with a proportion imported from elsewhere. This state of affairs began to end in the second half of the nineteenth century, when successive overseas conflicts disrupted production in Britain. In Australia, Canada, and South Africa efforts were made to become less dependent on outside supplies of manufactured goods, not least of glass. Searches were initiated for supplies of suitable sand, alkali, and fuel, and sites chosen as close as possible to all three. In most instances it was the brewers and the druggists who provided the impetus, and often also the capital, for the establishment of glasshouses that eventually supplied all needs.

An early, but faltering, start was made in Australia, when a man named Simeon Lord advertised in the *Sydney Gazette* for glass blowers. That was in May 1812; a month later it was stated in the same newspaper that 'upwards of a gross of perfect tumblers' had been produced. Lord is supposed also to have made bottles, but details are lacking, none surviving to confirm the possibility, and the venture failed not long after it had begun.

It was not until 1867 that successful manufacture started. In that year, James Ross established a glasshouse at Sydney, and two wholesale chemists, Alfred Felton and Frederick Grimwade, opened another at Port Melbourne, making bottles for their own requirements. After various changes of location and ownership the two firms combined in 1915 to become the nucleus of the Australian Glass Manufacturers Company, now Australian Consolidated Industries. The latter concern owns examples from both the Melbourne and Sydney factories, and displays them at Tooth's Brewery Museum, Broadway, Sydney.

A somewhat fuller record is available of bottle-making in Canada. A few bottles dating from 1855–60 are in the Royal Ontario Museum, Toronto, some of them authenticated by moulded inscriptions and others attributed on less convincing evidence. Factories opened and closed in many provinces after varying periods in operation, many of them being largely dependent on making utilitarian domestic articles like bottles. Only in a few instances, however, is there other than documentary record of such activity.

The Foster Brothers glass works, at St. Johns, Quebec, was started in 1855 and remained in operation for about a quarter-century, having been opened by two brothers from Boston, Massachusetts. A bottle of their manufacture is described by Gerald Stevens as being 'gourd shaped, with a pointed bottom', and about 25cm. in height: a Canadian version of the English Hamilton bottle. It is of a type stated to have been used in Quebec for spruce beer, a beverage made from steeped spruce shoots and yeast, gaseous, and therefore requiring a strong container with a constantly moistened cork to retain the contents in good condition.

In Ontario the Hamilton Glass Works, Hamilton, was established in 1865. A surviving bottle has a cylindrical body, sloping shoulders and blob lip. It bears in relief the retailer's name, 'Pilgrim Bros. & Co – Hamilton', and an eagle with outstretched wings. In the same town the Burlington glass works was started ten years later, closing in 1909. Stevens sought out one of the men who had worked there from 1885: the worker gave him much information as well as examples of the output. Some of these were confirmed by fragments found on the factory site, including ink bottles and other small bottles.

42

South African bottle-making followed the same patterns as those described above. In 1879 the South African Glass Co. Ltd. was registered, announcing that its output would range 'from the finest to the roughest'. Despite this willingness to meet all demands, it closed after only three years. Some examples of its products are in the Castle Museum, Cape Town. After the turn of the century there were unsuccessful attempts to start glassworks near Simonstown and Pretoria, the latter producing bottles both by hand-blowing and by machinery. A further essay took place at Durban during the 1914–18 War, when there was an acute shortage of pharmacy bottles in the country. The venture proved viable, was moved to Talana, Natal, and under the aegis of South African Breweries eventually grew into a flourishing business. Since then, further large works have been built at Wadeville, Transvaal, and Bellville, Cape Province. The combine of Consolidated Glass Works Ltd. produces nearly 1,500 million bottles and containers a year, enough to fill the needs of South Africa and with a surplus for export.

English Wine Bottles

The term 'wine bottle' is generally understood to mean one holding a quart (1·137 litres), although others of half that capacity or of greater size were made and used. In all instances the amount of liquid content could only be approximate in the days of mouth-blown examples, because it was impossible to obtain complete standardization. This desirable goal was not achieved until the nineteenth century, when machinery took over from the craftsman. The majority of the bottles were made of what was termed, and still is termed, 'black glass', although the material is either a dark brown or a shade of green that can barely be distinguished in reflected light. Further, the very word 'wine' can be no more than guesswork, as the bottles could have held liquids of many kinds, but it is convenient to employ it in view of the likelihood that in most instances it is correct.

The earliest mention of the manufacture of such wine bottles in England was the subject of controversy. In 1662 two glassmakers, Henry Holden and John Colinet (or Colnet), were granted a patent for having 'invented and attained unto the perfecting of making glass bottles.' A condition of the privilege was that the bottles were of sizes to hold stated quantities, and that each should bear Colinet's 'particular stamp or mark'. No example fitting the description has yet been discovered, probably for the reason that none were made because the patent was withdrawn. The withdrawal occurred following complaints from other glassmakers that Colinet had not invented the bottles, and that they had been in use for over thirty years. It was stated that Colinet did no more than make and supply bottles that were the invention of Sir Kenelm Digby, the latter being a man whose career embraced many roles: author, diplomatist, and, by the standards of the day, scientist.

The possibility that Sir Kenelm might have had some connexion with the making of glass wine bottles gains credibility because of his known acquaintance with a fellow-Welshman, James Howell. Howell spent the early years of his career in the employ of Sir Robert Mansell, for whose London glasshouse he acted as manager, and then travelled on the mainland of Europe on Mansell's behalf. While abroad he purchased at Alicante supplies of barilla, a soda used by the Venetians and the English for their best glass, and in Venice arranged the sending of craftsmen to London. It was after he left the industry that Howell met Digby, and the two became friends. So much so, that Sir Kenelm's 'Sympathetic Powder', a preparation that cured by merely being applied to a bandage removed from a wound and retained with the powder until the wound healed, had its allegedly successful trial by Howell in about 1624. Thus, Digby was on good terms with a man who had a practical knowledge of glass and its making, and could have assisted him on the subject of bottles.

Although it is not improbable that Digby invented or inspired the English wine bottle, positive evidence of his connexion with it has not been found. In his favour are the testimony of the men who objected to the 1622 patent application, and his interest in scientific matters and in wine-making.

An indication that the bottle was in being, with or without the aid of Digby, at the pertinent date, about 1632, may lie in Customs records of the time. What were described as 'English bottles' are noted by Eleanor Godfrey as having been exported to the Canary Islands in 1634 and 1640. There is a complication in the fact that the bottles, 100 dozen in 1634 and 260 dozen in 1640, were valued at £7 10s. and £19 10s. respectively. In both instances they were reckoned at 7½d. a dozen, suggesting that they were grossly undervalued, but this was not unusual where exporting and importing were concerned. The values were placed on goods by the Customs for assessing duty, figures sometimes bearing little resemblance to wholesale or retail prices, and this was more likely to be the case when a newly-introduced product was involved.

The foregoing is a brief outline of what is known or surmised about bottle-making in England during the early seventeenth century. While the great majority of the millions of bottles produced during the period have disappeared, enough of them have survived to demonstrate what they looked like in any one decade and how their appearance altered over the years. It has been possible to chart with reasonable accuracy the changes in shape because of the custom whereby an owner had his name, initials, or other personal marking placed on a bottle during manufacture. The date was sometimes included.

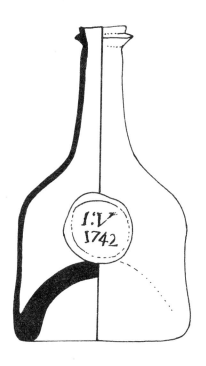

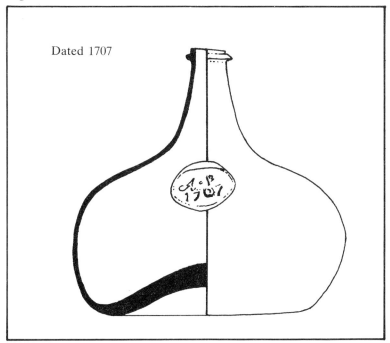

Dated 1707

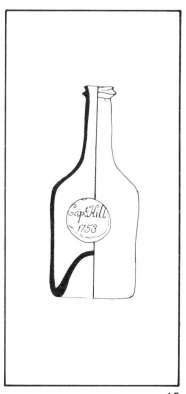

The earliest-known dated seal, detached from its bottle, is inscribed 'John Jefferson 1652' with a coat of arms, and is in the Museum of London. Contemporary with it or slightly earlier in date are two bottles found in London by Ivor Noël Hume, one of which is now in the Corning Museum of Glass, the other remaining with the finder. Each is sealed with the initials R W, exactly matching a detached seal excavated at Jamestown, Virginia, on land that once belonged to a colonist named Ralph Wormeley, who is thought to have died in 1651. It should be added that the foregoing examples were apparently eclipsed by a seal described as being attached to the base of a bottle excavated at Chester in 1939, and said to have borne the date 1562. It was recorded in print in 1948 and subsequently disappeared, so the surprisingly early date on the seal cannot be authenticated.

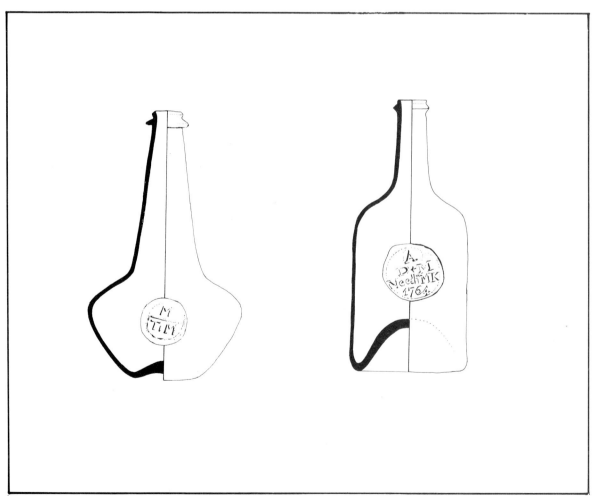

The early bottle shapes were given aptly descriptive names by W. A. Thorpe, who listed them as follows:

Shaft and globe: *c.* 1650, with a long neck and spherical body.
Onion: *c.* 1690, with a squat body and short neck, the latter scarcely long enough to provide a firm hand-grip.
Slope and shoulder: *c.* 1715–50, with a straight-sided body and a neck of a height about equal to that of the body.

By 1750, shapes had begun to become more or less standardized, with tall cylindrical bodies and medium-length necks, and a recognizable likeness to modern bottles.

In addition to the standard bottle and its ancestors, a number of unusual shapes have survived. Some of them are of oval section and have been called Bastard bottles, because many bear a seal with that surname, the Bastard family having been long-established in the west of Eng-

land. Another variant is the octagonally-bodied bottle, which was in production in the 1730s or earlier. In 1737 a Kent dealer advertised Newcastle 'eight-square' bottles for sale, and a dated sealed example of 1739 has been recorded. Others with later seals are known, including some of 1769 and 1770 found on the site of Williamsburg, Virginia. This has led to a suggestion that these last were of American manufacture, but there is no evidence to support the claim and it must be assumed that they were imported from England.

The cylindrically-bodied bottle perhaps replaced the clumsy onion shape because it was easier to handle; not only did the short neck make the earlier type difficult to hold when pouring, but the bulbous body gave it a lack of balance when tipped. In addition, the cylindrical bottle took up less space in storage, because it could be laid on its side. In this position the contents remained in contact with the cork and the latter, through being kept moistened, expanded to form an airtight seal. The wine inside was thus preserved until it was required.

It is probable also that the use of corks as closures played no small part in dictating bottle shape. Corks had been in use for the purpose since the early days of bottles, and excavated examples of pre-1700, still with firmly-placed corks protecting their contents, are not unknown. The first corks were conical in shape, fitted so that their tops projected above the bottle rims, and were held in place with packthread or wire.

The cork driven home flush with the bottle-rim would have been useless without the availability of a cork-screw. Such an accessory is mentioned in late-seventeenth-century documents, where it is referred to as a 'bottle-screw', but because it was not noticed earlier it cannot be assumed that it did not then exist. Awl-type tools were known, and required little adaptation to make them suitable for drawing corks; it is always unwise to underestimate the ingenuity of our forbears.

A growing liking for Port wine has been advanced as yet another reason for a change from the onion shape; a liking encouraged by the terms of the Methuen Treaty signed in 1703 by John Methuen, British envoy to the King of Portugal. The treaty allowed British woollen goods into Portugal in return for a lowering by one third of the duty on that country's wine compared with the rate charged on wines from elsewhere. With the lowering of its cost, there came a gradual increase in the consumption of Port in Britain.

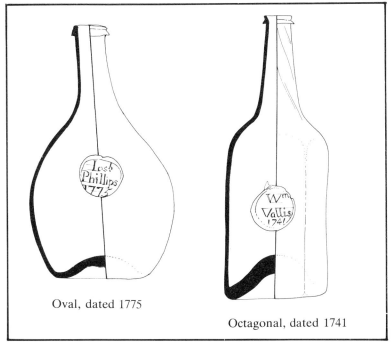

Oval, dated 1775

Octagonal, dated 1741

Flattened octagon, late 18th century

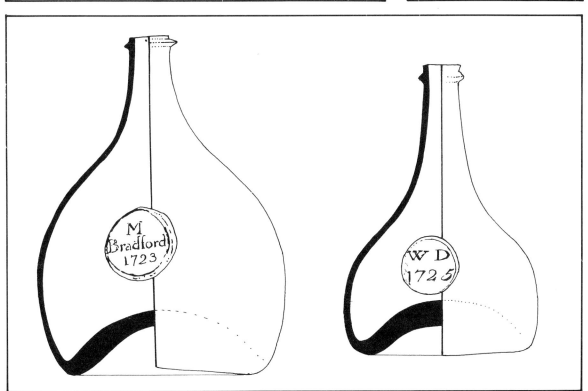

Port had been known and respected in England prior to 1703. It was first shipped in the 1670s, and in 1684 John Hervey, later first Earl of Bristol, purchased two hogsheads of the wine, which he continued ordering for the remainder of the century. Without doubt he was not alone in indulging a taste for it, so that when the wine became noticeably cheaper after 1703 there would have been a ready market for it.

The earlier shipments of Port were of a straightforward dinner wine, but later it was fortified with brandy and took its place with dessert. It was found that Port of this kind was very much to English tastes and that the best varieties of it improved with keeping. The result was that bottles of Port were matured carefully in cellars, where they lay on their sides keeping the corks expanded and economizing in space. It is debatable whether this treatment of the wine took place to any degree before the shape of the bottle had already altered for other reasons.

It would appear that the maturing of Port was by no means universal. In the records of All Souls College, Oxford, figures for the 1750s indicate that 'there should have been no Port more than eighteen months old in the cellars'. Likewise, a passage in a letter written in 1752 by Henry Purefoy, of Shalstone, Buckinghamshire, to his London wine-merchant demonstrates that he, too, was unconcerned about maturing his Port, but was anxious to keep it in drinkable condition. The letter was written on 27 December 1752, and runs, in part:

> The last red port of yours wch remains in Bottles – the corks faill & some of it is worsted, I should be glad to know what quantity of rosin & other stuff is used to make a Liquid to dip the head of the Bottles in after they are corked to prevent the Evaporating. Most people who come here drink white wine so I would endeavour to keep the red port good in the Bottle, because of its being kept a good while.

Purefoy was obviously not worried about a possibility of improving the wine in storage, but only to prevent it from turning sour.

A householder could, like Purefoy, have his bottles filled by a vintner from a selected cask, and would then have a quantity of them sent to his home. Likewise, the vintner would fill bottles of his own. In either instance, the preservation of the wine in good and clean condition was achieved, and it was ready for the table once the cork was drawn. So that each man, householder or trader, could immediately recognize his own property, he would have his bottles specially made with an identifying seal on each.

The Beilby and Bewick records, previously mentioned in connexion with bottle-moulds, also reveal important information about seals. Both men, and their successors, engraved them, listing each under the heading of 'marks'. Of the numerous examples recorded in the firm's accounts, very few indeed can be traced to existing bottles. The fact that so many were done and have subsequently vanished is not surprising in view of the knowledge that All Souls College bought some 10,000 bottles between 1749 and 1751, of which there seem now to be no trace whatsoever.

In most instances the procedure was for a glasshouse to order the seal on behalf of a customer. It would seem that a seal was not re-used should there be a repeat order, but one was engraved afresh even if the inscription on it was to be identical. Perhaps this was because after they had fulfilled an order with one, the metal die was ground down ready for re-cutting.

It is to be noted that in a few instances an order was givexn for a seal bearing a date differing from that when the work was done. For example, the accounts note that on 28 January 1804 three marks were to be engraved, lettered respectively: 'C. Case Tofts 1803', 'E. Case Redham 1806', and 'L. Case Pinkney 1804'. Again, in 1798 a seal was cut 'R. Pink 1796', and in 1804 one was engraved 'Wm. Green Takenham [Fakenham, Norfolk] 1806'.

The identified Newcastle bottles are so far insufficient in number to provide clues as to a particular feature that might assist in identifying others from the same source. Such points as the finish of lips and the lettering and devices on seals might be expected to suggest a common origin, but as yet the identified examples are too few to permit conclusions to be reached. At least it is now possible to attribute with confidence a number of bottles to a particular glasshouse, something that had hitherto only been possible with those made after 1822.

Among the few existing bottles that came from the Newcastle area are some that were made for Emmanuel College, Cambridge. Three separate orders for seal-engraving were recorded: in 1795, 1808, and 1828, all being on the instructions of Cookson's glasshouse, South Shields, who would have made the bottles. The same glasshouse had no less than twenty seals cut with G R or

From the fortress of Louis-bourg, Canada. Diameter 2.2 cm. (Parks Canada-Indian and Northern Affairs)

From St. Lawrence river fortifications, Canada, in use 1779-1856. Diameter 3.3 cm. (Parks Canada-Indian and Northern Affairs)

51

Richard Erisey, of Erisey,
Grade, Cornwall, died 1700

G R and a crown between 1796 and 1811. Seals detached from bottles and bearing the Royal initials have been found in many parts of the world where British troops were once stationed. For instance, at Fort Louisbourg, Nova Scotia, the fortress captured by the British from the French in 1745 and 1758 and finally destroyed.

The Cookson family also owned the Close Gate glass-houses, Newcastle, and ordered from Beilby and Bewick three seals for a Mr. I. S. Cann of Wymondham, Norfolk. One was engraved 'I. S. Cann Wymondham' and two bore the legend 'I. S. Cann Windham', rendering the place-name phonetically. The first of them was executed in 1802 and the others in 1805 and 1813; of the last-named there is a complete specimen in Strangers Hall Museum, Norwich. Two other bottles made for the same customer, but not listed by the firm of engravers, are in the Corning Museum of Glass, N.Y.; one is lettered 'I · S Cann 1794' and the other 'Cann Wymondham 1796.'

Revd. George Jeffery,
Vicar of Linkinhorne, Cornwall,
for 56 years, died 1780

Revd. Edward Giddy, of
St. Erth, Cornwall, died 1814

Revd. John Rouse, Rector
of Tetcott, Devon, 1816-17, died
1818

W. Williams, surgeon,
Llandovery, Dyfed

John Avery, perhaps
innkeeper at The Sun,
Winchester

John Griffiths, keeper of
The Mary Tavern, Cardiff

The oldest bottles surviving in quantity that can un-equivocally be given an origin are those made under the Ricketts patent. Not only do they bear on the shoulder the word 'PATENT', but beneath the base of each is moulded in raised letters, varying in legibility, the legend 'H. RIC-KETTS & CO. GLASSWORKS BRISTOL'. Specimens, which are sometimes sealed with an owner's name or other wording, were made from 1822 onwards. The words noted above encircle traces of a pontil-mark, but later examples, dating from the mid century, are lettered 'H·R BRISTOL' around a small central boss.

Henry Ricketts, with his father Jacob Wilcox Ricketts, leased their Bristol establishment, the Soap-Boilers' Glasshouse, Cheese Lane, St. Philip's, Bristol, in 1811. The name it bore was bestowed on it because it had been built as long ago as 1715 by a group of soap-makers, who doubtless entered the bottle trade as an outlet for the by-product of their industry: soaper's ash, an alkali of usc

Found on the beach at Hastings in 1898

The Packhorse, St. Blazey, Cornwall; an inn of that name survives there

Fox & Sons; the Fox family was prominent at Falmouth, Cornwall, as merchants. C. 1800

Frederick Latimer traded as a wine merchant. He took over his father's business in High Street, Oxford in 1846, and died probably in 1871

Needham Market, Suffolk

(Norfolk Museums Service)

St. Columb, Cornwall

John and Elizabeth Durell,
of Poole, Dorset

On a bottle thought to have
belonged to a member of the
Alles family, Guernsey,
Channel Islands

Sealed bottle made by Isaac
Cookson & Son, Newcastle
upon Tyne.

Margery Lethard; women's names are not often found alone on seals

Martin Lanyon, Liskeard, Cornwall; his Will was proved in 1734

The Will of Joseph Sturtridge, of Lostwithiel, Cornwall, was proved in 1778

No information

Bottles sealed only with a date are unusual

A merchant's mark, fore-runner of the modern trade mark, flanked by the numerals of the date; comparable seals have been excavated in Virginia

Hugh Pyper, of Tresmarrow, Cornwall, died in 1754 at the age of 83

The crest of an elephant's head is that of Eliot, of Port Eliot, St. German's, Cornwall

The arms are those of the Cary family

Crest, an anchor cabled

On a mottled glass bottle,
see plate 00

in glass-making. The style of the Ricketts firm was at first Ricketts, Evans and the Phoenix Glass Company, and then it became Henry Ricketts & Co. In 1853, after a brief period as Richard Ricketts & Co., it was amalgamated with an adjoining concern, Powells & Filer, of the Hoopers' Glasshouse, a move that terminated a long-established rivalry, and that was celebrated by a feast, 'the relation of whose mighty proportions was a favourite subject with some of the old men'. The amalgamation led to a change to Powells, Ricketts & Filer, and in 1856 to Powell & Ricketts. Under successive members of the Powell family the firm continued until 1919, and finally closed in about 1922.

The various styles under which the Ricketts firm traded from 1853 onwards were designated in full or by initials beneath the bases of their products. Soon after that date the pontil mark was no longer to be seen and was represented by a small boss where it would earlier have been visible. The Ricketts patent was not restricted to its inventor and Bristol, but would seem to have been licenced to at least one other glassmaker. A bottle is recorded with the usual 'PATENT' on the shoulder, and under the base 'WEAR GLASS Bo. Co. DEPTFORD'. The Wear Glass Bottle

Crest, a stork or a heron on
a cap of maintenance

A ducal coronet over the
initial 'R'

Crest and initials of Sir
Henry Carew, 7th Bt., of
Haccombe House, Newton
Abbott, Devon

Crest of Edgcumbe, of
Mount Edgcumbe, Cornwall.
19th century

A Robert Dugdale, of
Wareham, Dorset, was buried at
that town in 1766, aged 78

Company was established on the River Wear, at Deptford, a district of Sunderland, and was active from about 1814 to 1892.

The persons who used bottles embraced a wide range over the years. The earliest surviving complete, sealed bottle is dated 1657 and shows a crowned head with the initials 'R ^{P} M'. It is in the County Museum, Northampton, and was originally the property of the owners of a tavern named The King's Head. Many other bottles came from similar sources, those of Oxford having been the subject of considerable study, so that more is known about the bottles of the University city's inns than about any other group. The rôle of the local taverns in supplying drink to the colleges was a normal practice at Oxford, and was current from the second half of the seventeenth century until about 1750.

Recent investigation of the accounts of All Souls College have revealed much information on the subject as it affected that institution. Each tavern had its own bottles, sealed with its insignia, the initials of the owner or owners, and, often, a date. Thus, in 1685 Anne Morrell's seal showed her cypher, a crown for the name of her inn, the

Bideford, Devon; spelling was not a strong point with seal-engravers

Found by the Helford river, Cornwall

Thomas Rivers, The King's Head Inn, Truro

From Gelli Fud, Blackmill, Glamorgan

Thomas Grose, St. Kew, Cornwall

No information

Anne Morrell, 1679-96

Richard Walker, at The
King's Head, Oxford, 1687-1704

William and Anne Morrell,
at The Crown, Oxford, 1660-79

word 'OXON' and the date. Earlier, the Crown had been run by Anne Turton (1659–60), William and Anne Morrell (1660–79), and then by Morrell's widow on her own from 1679 to 1696.

Several of the city's taverns supplied the requirements of All Souls, and it was in 1661–2 that William Morrell of the Crown charged for six bottles of Claret. It is the first mention in the accounts of bottles in this connexion, while the rôle of the Three Tuns is confirmed by the finding of one of its sealed bottles in the College grounds in 1896.

Not only did the Fellows enjoy refreshment brought to their own premises, but it would appear that many of them foregathered elsewhere; then, as now. In 1733 it was remarked satirically that the College had transferred to the Three Tuns, as so many of the Fellows were to be seen there.

In the mid eighteenth century there came a change in practice: the Fellows started to buy wine and keep it readily available in their own cellars. It would seem that Exeter College, which had sealed bottles named and dated 1744, was the first to do this, and that All Souls followed suit within a few years. Plain bottles were employed at first, and then sealed ones followed with the letters 'A S C R' for All Souls Common Room. There were exceptions in the form of seals reading 'All: Souls College 1764', and 'All Souls Coll: C:R' (see Plates 19 and 20).

Jeremy Haslam has examined the thousand or so bottles remaining in the cellars, and concludes that with a few exceptions they all came from Mrs. Batchelor's glasshouse at Stourbridge. Each separate order was the subject of a freshly-cut seal, each varying from another in minor details, but several of them were obviously cut by the same hand.

The number of bottles used is perhaps surprising: in the 1950s about 6,000 were still there, but the number was later reduced by deliberate breakage to make space. Two centuries earlier it had been noted that the College possessed 587 dozen (7,044) bottles, which were thought to be a sufficient quantity.

Such prodigality was not especially remarkable. When the second Duke of Bedford was installed a Knight of the Garter in company with Prince George of Hanover and John Churchill, Duke of Marlborough, at Windsor in March 1702–3, there was a celebratory banquet in great style. The wines and beer sent down from London included Champagne and '12 dozen common Claret' as well as small ale, with the final item on the account being:

> Paid for nineteen dozen of bottles broken and lost and left with persons that had their fees of [in] wine   £2. 7. 6d.

How the bottles were obtained is not always easy to determine. All Souls at first ordered their supply direct from the glasshouse at Stourbridge, but from 1763 an Oxford china and glass dealer named Strange supplied them. As Stourbridge was the nearest glass-making centre it is likely that he got them from there, probably from the same maker as before.

No information

All Souls Common Room

On bottles used by benchers at the Inner Temple, 19th century

Going back in time, the Earl of Bedford used several sources in the late seventeenth century: the London maker Edmond Lewin vying with the city's two principal dealers, John Greene and Thomas Apthorpe, for his custom. Late in the 1660s Greene was in partnership with Michael Measey in the Strand, conveniently near the Earl's London mansion. During the next decade Greene traded on his own, with an address in the city: 'in the Poultry', a still-existing street leading out of Cheapside.

Less is known about Apthorpe, apart from the facts that he was a keen and successful businessman, and was Master of the Glass Sellers' Company in 1697 and 1698. Also in London, this time in 1663, Samuel Pepys, ever interested in following a fresh fashion, recorded in his diary on 23 October that he had been to see the filling of some of his new bottles 'made with my crest upon them'. The event took place at the Mitre tavern, kept by a man named Rawlinson, and it is possible that he had ordered the bottles on behalf of Pepys.

By the second half of the eighteenth century there were in London, and probably also elsewhere in the country, wholesale bottle merchants who may or may not have

Northmore Lawrence, mayor of Launceston, Cornwall, 1837-8

dealt with retail clients. One such firm was that of Rickman & Ross, 'at the Newcastle Bottle Warehouse, the bottom of Hungerford Market in the Strand'. The site of the market is now that of the Charing Cross hotel and railway station, and is commemorated by Hungerford Bridge, which carries trains and pedestrians over the Thames. The Warehouse was conveniently close to the river, so that bottles arriving from the North needed a minimum of transport on land. They would have been brought to the capital in coasters carrying coal and sheet glass, the latter being packed in special cases, as would have been the bottles. Richard Neve wrote in 1703 of the practice regarding sheet glass, and there can be little doubt that the cases of bottles were conveyed similarly surrounded by coal, 'by which means they are kept steady from falling and being broke by the motion, and rowling of the Ship'.

In 1774 Joseph Rickman, of the same address, was listed in a directory as a bottle and coal merchant, and in 1780 he appeared as a bottle merchant and mustard manufacturer. This combination of trades is not improbable when it is remembered that the best mustard of the day also came from the North: from Durham. At some date after 1780 Rickman took Ross into partnership, in 1807 the firm was styled Rickman, Ross & Rickman Jr., and it later became Rickman & Horne.

A surviving bill with Rickman & Ross's engraved heading, which incorporates the arms of Newcastle upon Tyne, is in the Joseph Downs Manuscript Collection at the Henry Francis du Pont Winterthur Museum, Delaware (56 x 5.43). It shows that between 27 June and 25 November 1788 Rickman & Ross supplied a nearby wine-merchant, Jonathan Michie, of 35 Craven Street, Strand, with 121 gross (17,424) of 'mould quart bottles'. At 36s. a gross or 3d. apiece the total sum involved was £217 16s., but with 15s. 3d. allowed for broken glass and 1s. 6d. a gross discount, the final total was £207 19s. 3d.

The price of bottles varied within narrow limits over the centuries. Records of the value of what quickly became commonplace domestic articles are comparatively few in number, but they shed a little light on life at various periods.

An early mention, which makes it plain that a glass bottle was intended and not one of pottery or stoneware, has been quoted by Ivor Noël Hume from the Expense-Book of James Master. It was printed in *Archaeologia Cantiana* in 1886 and read:

```
1657
July 2.    Paid for 10 bottles of Rhenish & 2 of sack   00 17 04
           Paid for 12 glasse bottles                    00 05 08
Aug. 20.   For 10 bottles of white wine & 2 of sack      00 08 10
           For 12 glasse quart bottles & corks           00 05 08
```

Hume also notes a gift made in 1651 of 'two doussen glasse bottles of the best Canary'.

In 1658 the fifth Earl of Bedford bought for use at his country seat, Woburn Abbey, 12 dozen glass bottles at 4s. 6d. a dozen. Presumably they were plain and quart-size, and the seller was Thomas Cross, a supplier of beer and ale. An account rendered to the same nobleman on 11 July 1671 refers unequivocally to quart glass bottles at 4s. 6d. a dozen, and then on 5 March 1671–2 he purchased:

12 doz of Glass bottles wth my Lords Coat on yem at 5^s p doz.

In 1672 the Earl purchased a further supply of sealed bottles in two separate batches, they totalled 18 dozen at a cost of 5s. 6d. a dozen. Later, in 1676, there were further orders for sealed bottles: in April for 18 dozen and three (219) again at 4s. 6d., and in the February (1676–7) for 8 dozen and 6 (102) of double-quart size at the same price; these last were known at the time as 'pottles'. Thenceforward orders were placed only for unsealed bottles, perhaps for the reason, suggested by W. A. Thorpe, that the Earl did not consider the extra cost of marking worthwhile. During the period 1671–91 the household ordered a total of 13,500 bottles, using them up at the rate of 700 a year. They were, therefore, no light expense, and a saving of a shilling a dozen, gained by dispensing with a seal, was a justifiable economy.

The Earl occasionally bought small quantities of pint bottles, one or two dozen at a time. They cost between 2s. and 3s. a dozen.

Further late-seventeenth-century records are in the accounts of Sir Thomas Myddelton, 2nd. Bt., of Chirk Castle, Denbighshire. On 7 February 1672–3 a payment of £2 was made to:

william wynne, the glass carrior, for 10 dozen bottles with yor name on.

A few years later Sir Thomas's accounts note a further

purchase. On this occasion, on 24 March 1679–80, the purchase was made from a local innkeeper:

> Payd Morris Jones, of wrexham, for 40 dozen of bottles to bottle cyder at my lord Cholmondeley, and at home at xxx^d p dozen
> £5.0.0.

In an effort to regulate their trade, a number of the London makers and sellers of bottles drew up in September 1680 a list of proposed prices. This was reprinted by W. A. Thorpe from the manuscript in the British Library (Sloane 857, 66 *obv.*) and is as follows:

> Pint bottles plain 2/6 per dozen
> Pint bottles marked 3/6 per dozen
> Quarte bottles pla 3/6 per dozen
> Quarte bottles mrd 4/6 per dozen
> Pottle bottles pla 7/– per dozen
> Pott. bott. mrd att 8/– per dozen
> Gall: Bott. pla: att 14/– per dozen
> Gall Bott mrd att 16/– per dozen
> Double Gall. plaine att 28/– per dozen
> Double Gall: mrd 32/– per dozen

In 1722 an advertisement printed in the Bristol *Freeholders' Journal* of 18 July gave the price of bottles, presumably quart-size, at 2d. apiece. It added: 'N.B. – The bottles are large and London-shaped'. The reference to 'London-shaped' presumably meant that there was nothing provincial about the appearance of the articles.

On two occasions in 1728 Wriothesley, 3rd Duke of Bedford, made purchases of bottles for his home, Thorney Abbey, Isle of Ely. On 27 July he bought 12 gallons of the imported spirit Arrack together with '4 dozen 2 bottles and basket,' the last items costing 11s. 4d. A few months later he obtained 6 gallons of Brandy and '2 dozen 1 bottles and corks', the latter at 4s. 5d. In both instances the quantities of spirits indicate quart bottles, and their price was roughly 2d. each.

They could be bought at slightly cheaper rates. For example the *Norwich Gazette* announced in November 1725:

> THIS is to acquaint all Persons, That there is to be sold at the Glass-House in South-Town near Yarmouth, a Sett of fine Quart Bottles at 20d. a Dozen, deliver'd at the Key belonging to the Works.

Two further advertisements confirm that bottles travelled by sea, as did most other goods prior to the building of railways. The first notice was in the *Ipswich Journal* for 13 July 1771:

> Glass Bottles will be sold until Michaelmas next at J. Stow's Bottle Warehouse on the Common Key, Woodbridge. Best Champagne Quarts at 24s. per gross or 2s. 1d. per doz. Common Quarts at 22s. per gross and 2s. per doz. Gentlemen may be supplied with square, octagon, or marked bottles, 'with names or arms' on shortest notice, all fruit bottles in proportion.

The other, earlier, notice in the *Kentish Post,* 12 June 1736, shows that southbound coasters called at the port of Faversham on the river Swale:

> Christopher Pratt of Feversham [*sic*] having a quantity of Newcastle Bottles, sells them to any person at a reasonable rate; Common Quarts at 18s. per groce; eight-square or long-necked quart bottles at 18s. per Groce; common pints at 14s., eight-square and long-necked pints at 16s., to be fetched from the Storehouse, and paid for.

It is noticeable that by the time the bottles reached the distant shores of America their price had advanced. Packing, long-distance transport, and agents' commission understandably had to be paid. Perhaps it is only to be expected that an advertiser in the *Boston Gazette* of 25 July 1763 offered 'NEWCASTLE QUART BOTTLES, at £15. per groce'. This works out at just a fraction over 2s. apiece. It may be recalled that Rickman and Ross, of the Newcastle Bottle Warehouse, sold them in 1788 at 3d. each, with a discount of 1s. 6d. a gross.

Mineral-water, Pharmacy, and Other Bottles

Beer Bottles

The earliest story about beer being kept in bottles, rather than in casks, concerns the long-lived Dr. Alexander Nowell, Dean of St. Pauls from 1560 until his death in 1602 at the age of about 95. A keen angler, he once accidentally left a bottle of beer on a river bank. Some days later the Dean returned to find it there, opening it to discover that it was 'no bottle, but a gun, so great was the sound at the opening thereof'. It is far from certain that the bottle in question was made of glass, and the date suggests that it was of Rhenish stoneware.

Glass bottles made specifically to hold beer were not made until late in the nineteenth century. Prior to that, the beverage was put into wine bottles. The nineteenth-century examples are of interest because they so often bear moulded names and locations, and can provide local historians with information about former inhabitants, industries, and buildings in an area.

Bitters Bottles

Bitters are alcoholic beverages flavoured with herbs and other ingredients and were popular during the nineteenth century. They were sold ostensibly as cures for all kinds of ailments, and for that reason were free of the prevailing high duties on alcohol; they enabled those with a taste for stimulants to pay lip-service to temperance while satisfying their craving and their conscience. Although well known in England, the greatest demand for bitters was in America, where movements for regulating the sale and imbibing of strong drink were very active, finally attaining their goal of complete prohibition.

18 Ink bottles (left to right): 'umbrella' shape; lettered UNDERWOOD'S INKS; domed with offset neck. American, late 19th century, heights 6.8cm., 7.3cm. and 3.8cm.

19 Sealed A*S C*R for All Souls Common Room, Oxford. Early 19th century, height 28cm.

20 Painted and gilt with a named portrait bust of Admiral Lord Nelson, and lettered CARRAWᵞ. Early 19th century, height 30.7cm.

21 Sealed All Souls College 1764. Height 25.3cm.

22　Octagonal bottle sealed Jn°
Andrews 1770. Height 23.1cm.

23　Flattened octagon sealed Row^d
Veale Gwithian 1778. Height 27.2cm,
base 11.6×8.1cm. Gwithian is in
Cornwall

24　Left, sealed Thomas Bolitho 1819,
height 27cm.; right, sealed Sam¹Archer
and marked beneath the base H. RIC-
KETTS & CO GLASS WORKS BRIS-
TOL, *circa* 1822, height 26.4cm.

25　Sealed bottle 1791.
　　Height 17.8cm.

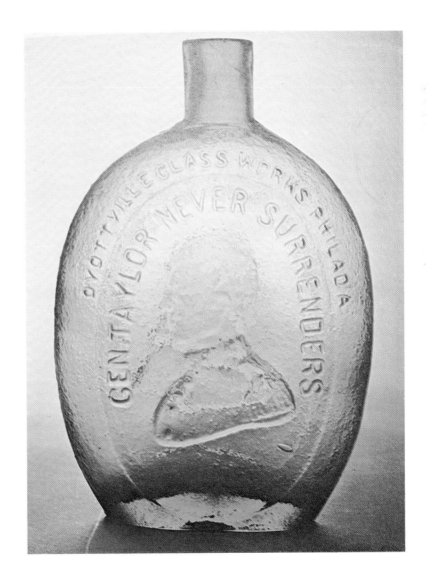

26 Spirit flask bearing a portrait of General Zachary Taylor bordered by the legend GEN. TAYLOR NEVER SUR-RENDERS and DYOTTVILLE GLASS WORKS PHILADA. American, height 17cm.

27 Corked wine bottle with contents intact, excavated at York. *Circa* 1700, height 16.1cm.

28 Sealed T M 1700. Height 17cm. Found in the sand at Hastings, 1898

29 Sealed M over T M. *Circa* 1650, height 23.1cm.

30 Iridescent wine bottle of small capacity. Mid–17th century, height 15cm.

31 Sealed T L 1686, the neck with a silver rim of later date. Height 17.7cm.

32 Two pharmacy bottles or phials.
17th century, heights 15.5cm. and
13.7cm.

33   Cologne bottles, the centre one with
its original printed paper label. Length
23.9cm.

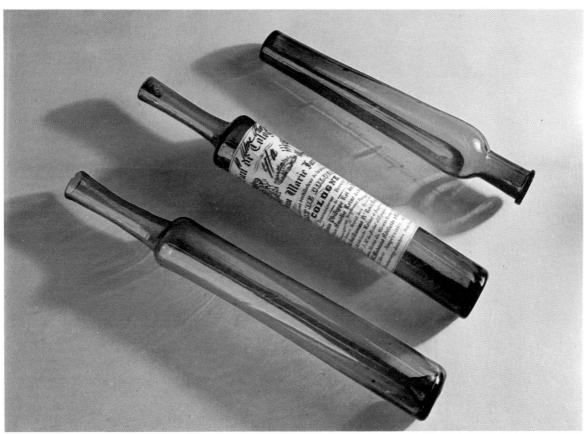

34 Perfume or Cologne bottle moulded with flowers. American, mid-19th century, height 10.8cm.

35 Codd bottles lettered (left) GROVES & WHITNALL LTD. SALFORD and REDFEARN BOTTLE MAKERS BARNSLEY, height 22.3cm; and (right) RANDALL BRO⁵ EPSOM & ADDLESTONE and Reliance Patent Sole Maker Dan Rylands Barnsley, height 21.5cm.

36 Chemist's storage jar with metal
cover. 19th century, height overall 33cm.

37 Sealed Trengoff in Cornwell 1704. Height 13.5cm. The manor of Trengoff is in the parish of Warleggan, Cornwall

Flattened oval bottle sealed Ʌich: Brown 1716. Height 18.1cm.

40 Sealed DVO 1724. Height 17.5cm.

38 Sealed J: Lowther Esq ʳUpleatham 1734. Height 21.9cm. Upleatham is a village in Cleveland

39 Iridescent bottle. *Circa* 1730, height 26cm. Dredged from a lock near Ipswich in 1974

The innumerable varieties of bitters were each sold in a distinctive bottle, many of which bore moulded inscriptions and insignia, and all had printed labels proclaiming their virtues. The shapes and colours of the bottles were as diverse as their contents and as the claims of their makers

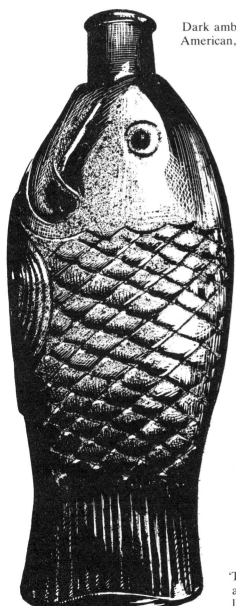

Dark amber bitters bottle. American, 1870s, height 25 cm.

'The Great Tonic', dark amber bitters bottle. American, late 19th century, height 32.4 cm.

65

Cardevines and Large Bottles

Confusion appears to have occurred in the use of the word cardevine or gardevine. It meant a big-bellied bottle of unspecified capacity, or a case, chest, or cellar for wine bottles. There was also a word gardeviance, meaning a food container, that was sometimes used interchangeably with cardevine. Thus, Richard Boyle, first Earl of Cork, noted in his diary in 1628: 'This day receaved . . . a gardeviance of usqubag', presumably meaning that he had been sent a case of whisky. He does not say if it was in glass bottles, but this is not improbable. In 1621 the accounts of Lord William Howard, of Naworth Castle, recorded the purchase of '2 bottles, to put wine in, 8d.', and in 1624 there was the entry 'For 2 sellers, with glasseis of 8 pottils a peace 26s.' There is no proof, however, that any of these bottles were of English manufacture.

In 1759 Knight & Co., of the 'New Glass-house, near the Salt House Dock, Liverpool, advertised 'cardevin bottles, &c.' In March 1769 the same firm offered for sale 'all sorts of gardevine[s,] squares and bottles', and later in that year Peter Morris & Sons, at the same address, could supply 'cardevines, squares, &c.'

Shrewton, near Stonehenge, Wiltshire. Large capacity, height 33.4 cm., diameter 17.2 cm.

Like the cardevine, the demi-john was large and round and its capacity was similarly undefined. It could be anything between two and twelve gallons, with a supposed average of five gallons. The glass vessel was encased in wicker with one or two woven carrying-handles. The demi-john traditionally acquired its name from the French *Dame Jeanne,* but it is not clear who this good lady may have been or when she lived.

Use of the demi-john was not confined to Europe. An advertisement in the *Columbian Centinel* of 17 December 1788 announced that the Pitkin Glass Works, Connecticut, would supply the public with 'dime-johns or any other large bottles'.

A number of terms have gained currency with reference to oversize containers for wine, varying from one district to another. A modern list of them shows the variations in the Bordeaux and Champagne vineyards:

CAPACITY	BORDEAUX	CHAMPAGNE
2 bottles	Magnum	Magnum
3 ,,	Marie-Jeanne	
4 ,,	Double Magnum	Jeroboam
6 ,,	Jeroboam	Rheoboam
8 ,,	Imperial	Methuselah
12 ,,		Salmanazar
16 ,,		Balthazar
20 ,,		Nebuchadnezzar

Large bottles include carboys: the oversized globular glass bottle used for the transport of acids and other liquid chemicals. Carboys were given a woven wicker covering to safeguard them from damage, but in recent years this protection has sometimes been stripped away so that the carboy can be used as an 'indoor garden'.

Case Bottles

The case bottle is rectangular in section, slightly wider at the shoulders than at the base, and with a very short neck having an out-turned rim. Invariably they are made of a green metal, and frequently exhibit bubbles and other imperfections (Plate 7). The bottles can date back to the early seventeenth century, and earned their name from being transported in cases, known also as 'chests' or 'cellars'. Traditionally, the case bottle is supposed to have held gin, but this was not invariably so and they were sometimes used for other liquids. However, in support of the tradition is the modern appellation 'Old Square Face' used by a Dutch gin distiller.

The shape described above applies to bottles that ranged in size up to 40cm. in height. Smaller examples were of square section without a taper, and all were occasionally sealed. In some instances closures took the form of corks or, commonly up to about 1750, pewter caps. These were threaded on the inside, and screwed on to a threaded pewter ring affixed to the neck of the bottle. In most examples the metal is thinly blown, and especially on the large bottles curves inwards in the side panels. Many bear marks moulded beneath their bases: crosses, rosettes, and so on, and with some exceptions originated on the mainland of Europe.

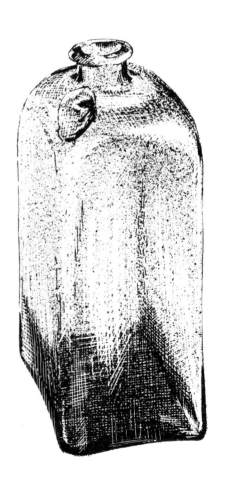

Pale green sealed case bottle. French, 18th century, height 18 cm.

Seal on case bottle

Gum and Ink Bottles

Small quantities of gum and ink were sold in glass bottles. The majority were of poor-quality glass, bluish or greenish in colour, bubbled, and with lips sheared and re-heated to form a crude finish. Many of them therefore have a deceptive appearance, looking much older than they are and defying accurate dating. Although most bottles for holding these liquids were of straightforward pattern, a few were more ingenious. Sellers of ink realized that their customers disliked waste, and some of their products were sold in specially shaped bottles to obviate this. They were designed to rest at an angle so that the last drop of ink, or almost the last drop, was accessible and a minimum remained unused.

Bottle probably for gum. Height 6.3 cm.

Ink bottle, lettered BLACKWOOD & Co PATENT LONDON. Diameter 4.5 cm.

Pale blue-green ink bottle with pen-rests, initialled under base P:C. Height 6 cm.

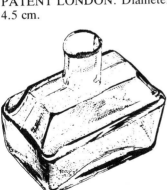

Pale green ink bottle with pen-rests. Height 5.9 cm.

Tilting ink bottle, shown tilted. Height 6.5 cm.

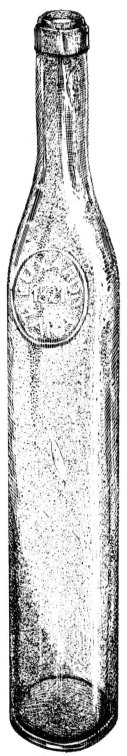

Pale green liqueur bottle
sealed LUXARDO ZARA 1821.

Household Bottles

Many household products were sold in glass bottles. Each of them once bore a printed paper label naming the contents, but when this is missing identification is often a matter of guesswork. Late-nineteenth and twentieth-century examples can be more helpful, as in many instances they are moulded in relief with a maker's name, a brand name, or some other indication. The bottles were used for such varied commodities as sauces, vinegar, oil, boot blacking, and ammonia; in fact, for anything suitable for pouring from a narrow-mouthed container. Household bottles were made in all shapes, sizes, and colours, each user packing his product in a way that he hoped would catch the eye of the customer.

Liqueur Bottles

For many decades it was customary to put liqueurs in strictly functional bottles. The plainest of them being used by the sellers of long-established liqueurs, including brandies; brandies are still displayed in bottles of French eighteenth-century 'flower-pot' shape. In contrast to them is the tall square or cylindrical glass bottle used for the cherry liqueur, Maraschino. The drink was first produced at Zara, capital of Dalmatia, once a part of the Austro-Hungarian Empire and now in Yugoslavia. The Maraschino bottles most often seen are of a bright-green metal with a moulded seal on the upper front, and dating from the late nineteenth century. The seal includes the name of the maker of the contents, 'ZARA', and the Austrian eagle.

Milk Bottles

Cows' and goats' milk was first sold ready-bottled in the third quarter of the nineteenth century. Prior to that time, and continuing to within living memory, town housewives or their servants brought their jugs to the itinerant milkman, who pushed along each street, from house to house, a small hand-cart holding a metal churn. The contents of the churn was ladled-out to each customer, the milk being exposed to the germ-laden open air.

The late-nineteenth-century innovation of delivering milk that had been measured into bottles at a central depôt took place on both sides of the Atlantic. The availability of comparatively cheap containers and a general desire for higher standards of hygiene coincided, but it was several decades before laws were drafted making it compulsory for all milk to be bottled before sale.

Dr. Harvey D. Thatcher's 'Milk Protector'. American, *c.* 1890, height 33.2 cm.

In England it is thought that George Barham, founder of a chain of dairies, the Express Dairy Company, initiated the sale of bottled goats' milk in 1884. The glass container or its contents, or both, did not have a sufficient appeal for the public and the project was abandoned. A few years later other attempts were made to supply cows' milk in the same manner, and in 1894 a north-country dairyman, Anthony Hailwood, offered his customers sterilized milk in bottles with swing-stoppers.

Later came a waxed disc fitting into a groove moulded just below the neck-rim: a quick and inexpensive closure that was widely used. It suffered the drawback that the top edge of the bottle was unprotected against infection, which would be transmitted to the milk when pouring it out. This was overcome by changing to a card cap, shaped so that it completely covered the top of the bottle, with its crimped sides held in place by a metal ring. Later again came the metal foil cap that was easily pressed into a groove on the outside of the bottle rim. In addition to changes in design of the neck to accommodate the various closures, the bottles themselves altered in shape over the years. Many bore the supplier's name moulded in relief, and this was superseded by printing it in fired colours.

In the United States bottled milk is said to have been sold in Brooklyn in 1878, and soon afterwards a number of bottles designed for the purpose were marketed. In 1884 a clear-glass bottle with a glass top held in place by a wire bail was invented by Dr. Harvey D. Thatcher. The bottle was named on its side 'The Milk Protector' and bore a representation in relief of a farmer seated on a stool and milking a cow. Thatcher duly turned his attention to using a paper or card closure, and others from 1900 onwards experimented with the use of square bottles. A belief that exposure to daylight might be injurious to milk occasionally led to the public's preference for clear glass being ignored. In 1929 a Massachusetts farmer tried selling his product in a green glass bottle and a few tried with dark amber, but such ventures were not successful.

Mineral-water Bottles
The healing properties of natural mineral waters were highly appreciated in the past, when almost every country boasted one or more spas at which visitors 'took the cure'. Spa, near Liége, Belgium, is supposed to be one of the

oldest on the mainland of Europe, and to have given its name to all the others. The various waters were recommended for the cure or alleviation of many ailments, and prescribed amounts were bravely swallowed by the truly sick as well as by *malades imaginaires*. Many of the visitors gained relief from their suffering, while those in good health gathered at the spas from time to time as part of the routine of fashionable life.

In eighteenth-century England Tunbridge Wells and Bath were in the forefront, but many other places, large and small, achieved status as spas. Among them was Scarborough, Yorkshire, to which the redoubtable Sarah Churchill, Duchess of Marlborough, journeyed in 1732 in an effort to cure her gout and other disabilities.

Arriving at her destination after a lengthy coach journey, the Duchess lost little time in reporting to her favourite grand-daughter what she thought of the place. Sweeping condemnation is in every paragraph of the letter: the town, the food, the people, all were a disappointment. From her description of the room in which ladies took the waters it would seem that her complaint in that particular was justified:

> there is nothing but hard narrow benches, which is rather a punishment to sit upon than an ease. When the waters begin to operate, there is a room within it, where there is above twenty holes with drawers under them to take out and all the ladies go in together and see one another round the room, when they are in that agreeable posture, and at the door, there's a great heap of leaves which the ladies take in with them.

Not surprisingly, Sarah was affronted at the sight, and in her next letter wrote suggesting that there was probably little difference should she drink the waters in the room at Scarborough or elsewhere. She added:

> I believe this terrible journey will end in only seeing a great quantity bottled up and taking them to drink at some of my houses, which will be a sad conclusion to go four hundred miles over places I believe worse than the Alps, only to fetch water.

Later, still at Scarborough in spite of its shortcomings, the Duchess was able to say that the waters had benefited her. Nevertheless, she was determined that she would never again set foot in the town:

> if the waters happen to do me good, as they have the same effect in my lodging, as when I go to the well, I will have them bottled up carefully, putting oil upon the top and then wax upon the cork.

Adding a little oil to each filled bottle would have assisted in keeping it airtight. From this, it would appear that the bottles were to travel and be stored in an upright position; if laid on their sides the oil would have served no purpose. Although it is probable that the Duchess used bottles made of glass, their material is not specified.

At about the same date water from Bristol Hotwells was available for those wanting to take it in their own homes, and again there is a doubt about containers. An advertisement in the *Freeholders' Journal* published in Bristol on 18 July 1722 announced 'Bristol water for sale in Bottles'. A few years later, however, Defoe clarified the position when he wrote:

> There are no less than fifteen Glass-Houses in Bristol. . . . They have indeed a very great Expence of Glass Bottles, by sending them fill'd with Beer, Cyder, and Wine to the West Indies, much more than goes from London; also great Numbers of Bottles, even such as is almost incredible, are now used for sending the Waters of St. Vincent's Rock away, which are now carry'd, not all over England only, but, we may say, all over the World.

Later in the century there was a further mention in Matthews's Bristol directory for 1793–4. In a survey of the city's trade, the writer noted 'The great demand for glass bottles for the Bristol Water'.

Travellers to distant countries were also wont to return with supplies of ready-bottled waters, or were able to purchase them in London and elsewhere. Both in England and America such bottles have been discovered, their shapes proclaiming a foreign origin and in some instances their contents being indicated on seals, for example: 'PIERMONT WATER' or 'Pyrmont Water', and 'POUHON-IN-Spa'; the former from Germany, and Pouhon being the name of the spring from which waters were taken at Spa, Belgium. Among recorded examples of old Pouhon-in-Spa bottles is one that was found embedded in the wall of a house at Ramsbury, Wiltshire, and another recovered from the bed of the River Severn. Pyrmont bottles have been excavated on the site of Colonial Williamsburg, Virginia.

If Americans imported European waters, in due course they were able to enjoy the benefits of those of their own country. Here also was a choice of attending in person or buying the water bottled. Saratoga Springs, not far from New York, was opened at the end of the eighteenth century, and the bottled product was put on sale in about 1820. Thirty years later more than 7,000,000 bottles of the water were sold in a year and the output increased as the century progressed. Also well known was the water from Poland Springs, near Portland, Maine, opened in 1860. A few years later the public was offered the water in bottles modelled to resemble the prophet Moses, 'who brought thee forth water out of the rock of flint'.

Few fashionable persons in eighteenth-century Europe did not pay one or more visits to a spa during a lifetime, but they were expensive places and only the wealthier could afford to patronize them. By the end of the century it became possible to make the waters artificially and bring their benefits to a wider range of the public.

The commercial manufacture of these mineral waters was due to the researches of a number of men of different nationalities. Their work was adapted and put into practice by Joseph Priestley, the English chemist whose other accomplishments embraced the Nonconformist ministry and radical politics. With others of his contemporaries he investigated the properties of what was then called 'fixed air', and in 1772 published *Directions for impregnating water with fixed air . . . to communicate the peculiar Spirit and Virtues of Pyrmont Water*. In simple terms, he showed how to put the tiny bubbles of gas into water and give it the appearance of natural spring water. In his memoirs he wrote: 'I can make better than you import, and what cost you five shillings will not cost me a penny'. It was the French chemist, Lavoisier, who demonstrated that the 'fixed air' was composed of oxygen and carbon: a mixture now known as carbon dioxide or carbonic acid gas.

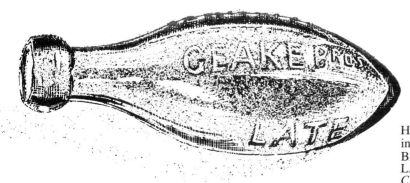

Hamilton bottle invented in about 1809, lettered GEAKE BROs LATE J.S. EYRE LAUNCESTON ESTABd 1820. *C.* 1890, length 19.1 cm.

75

By 1781 a Manchester apothecary was marketing a variety of artificial mineral-waters, including one that became known as soda water. A dozen years later a German, Jacob Schweppe, who had established a mineral-water manufactory at Geneva in 1789, extended his operations to London. In 1793 he was selling his brand of Seltzer water, made in imitation of the product of the springs at Nieder-Selters, near Koblenz, Germany, and later gained a reputation for his soda water. It was as 'Soda Water Manufacturers' that the firm of Schweppe & Co., 79 Margaret Street, Cavendish Square, appeared in a London directory of 1821.

Glass bottles that were both strong and attractive in appearance were favoured for holding the waters. The drawback to them, and likewise to those of pottery, was that the corks used as closures were apt to allow the gas to leak away. A report dated 1802 stated that both pottery and glass were then in use for the purpose, but no details were given of the latter.

In 1812 the Newcastle glasshouse of Isaac Cookson & Sons ordered a brass mould to be engraved by the Beilby and Bewick workshop with the wording 'Clapham & Co. Mineral Water Newcastle'. Again, as no example appears to have survived, the type of bottle cannot be determined. However, clearer evidence exists in the case of William Hamilton of Dublin, who carefully described a bottle in a patent granted to him in 1809.

The patent was for 'A new mode of Preparing Soda and other Mineral Waters'. In the specification Hamilton remarks, almost as an aside, that

> I generally use a glass or earthen bottle of a long ovate form, . . . not having a square bottom to stand upon, it can only lie on its side, of course, no leakage of air can take place, the liquid matter always being in contact with the stopper.

Hamilton added that the shape gave strength to the containers, and that he tied the corks in place but sometimes used closures of other materials. It has been suggested that the Hamilton 'egg' or 'torpedo' bottle may have been in use for some years prior to 1809, and Olive Talbot mentions a tradition that it was devised in the first place by Nicolas Paul, an early associate of Schweppe who established a concern of his own in London in 1802.

A small number of early egg bottles has been recorded, each with a narrow out-turned lip and a pontil mark on the slightly flattened base. Later examples were given a rounded 'blob' lip and lack a pontil mark. The practicality of the bottles was proved by their remaining in favour for over a century, only ceasing to be produced in about 1914.

It must have been at some date prior to the mid century that it was found that what Defoe called a taste of 'the Allom' was not to the taste of the multitude, but that aerated water flavoured with fruit-juice or spices and syrup was more attractive. The sale of such preparations, and all other goods in glass bottles, was greatly increased after the repeal of the duty on glass in 1845. Thus, when it was decided that the refreshment contractors at the Great Exhibition of 1851 must sell no alcoholic drinks whatsoever, the egg bottle and others, with their contents, came into their own. The Exhibition was open for 141 days, from 1 May to 11 October inclusive, and during that period was visited by an average of 42,000 persons a day. The grand total of 6,039,195 would seem to have found viewing the exhibits a thirsty business. They consumed 1,092,337 bottles of Schweppe's soda-water, lemonade, and ginger-beer, and 5,350 bottles of a beverage named 'Masters' Pear Syrup'.

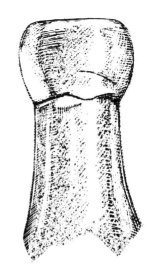

'Blob' lip. 19th century, maximum diameter 3.3 cm.

Although the flavoured drinks were quite unlike anything that flowed from a natural source, they continued for many decades to be termed mineral-waters, a name they still retain alongside the more accurate alternatives, aerated or carbonated waters. However, not everyone pandered to a sweet-tooth, and many remained faithful to spring waters and their imitations. To cater for this minority Messrs. Struve & Co., of the Royal German Spa, Brighton, which had been initiated by Dr. F. A. Struve in 1825, displayed their products at the Exhibition. In the *Official Catalogue* they were described in these words:

> Artificial mineral waters, of similar composition to the springs at Spa, Pyrmont, Marienbad, Kissingen, Seltzer, Fachingen, Püllna, and Vichy. The factitious chalybeates are said to contain the carbonate of iron in solution, whereas in those imported, a part, or the whole is precipitated.

Seltzer water and others were often retailed in a short bright-green cylindrical bottle, referred to as a 'dumpy', moulded with the supplier's name and sometimes that of the contents. Alternatively, taller and slimmer bottles, small versions of wine bottles, were used. All were sealed with corks, usually wired to hold them in place.

Substitutes for the unreliable cork were actively sought. One of the earlier of them was patented in 1869 by two men from St. Helier, Jersey, Henry Barratt and John Adams. Their simple device was a short wooden dowel grooved to hold a rubber washer; the wood had to be heavier than water so that it sank when the top of the plug was pressed, and the gas-pressure holding it in place was released. *Lignum vitae,* a timber brought from the West Indies and South America, was found to be particularly suitable, being of the required density and impervious to moisture.

'Codd' bottle, lettered HICKS ST. AUSTELL and SWG (for South Wales Glass Company, Newport), with internal screw to neck. Height 22 cm.

Mid-green 'dumpy' bottle, lettered Dr STRUVES MINERAL WATERS, used for water from the German Spa, Brighton, Sussex. 19th century, height 14.4 cm.

The most popular and intriguing container used for aerated waters was the one initially patented in 1870 by Hiram Codd, of Camberwell, London. He was a manufacturer of soda water, as well as of a beverage felicitously referred to as 'temperance champagne'. Codd used a glass 'marble' captive inside the bottle, because it was larger than the neck diameter, and sealed by the gas-pressure holding the marble up against a rubber washer just inside the rim. The contents were released by pushing on the top of the marble with a turned wood cap, allowing the gas to escape and the marble to fall out of the way.

'Moses' bottle for Poland Springs water. American, *c.* 1880, height 29.2 cm.

Hiram Codd's 'Bulb' bottle, patented in 1885

Dan Rylands 'Reliance', patented in 1885

Variants of Hiram Codd's original patented design of 1870

Schoolchildren were understandably fascinated by the small glass ball rolling about inside the emptied bottle, and untold thousands were smashed to obtain the marble. The bottles were intended for re-use after cleaning; with lemonade and other drinks sold in country areas for as little as 1½d., there could have been little or no profit when a bottle's life was terminated abruptly after only one or two fillings. Little or nothing could be done, however, to lessen the temptation, and the glass ball remained an irresistible prize for the young.

Codd's first version allowed the marble to drop to the bottom of the bottle when the pressure was released. In this it shared the defect of Barrett's plug; in both instances the closures tended to re-seal automatically as pouring took place. A year after he had introduced the bottle, Hiram Codd was granted a further patent for his idea of pinching the neck so that the ball moved in a confined space and was trapped as the bottle was tipped. Additional factors in favour of the new version were that the glass ball was easy to keep clean and the rubber washer could be removed easily for replacement. The Barrett plug, on the other hand, could not be prevented from impeding pouring, was comparatively unhygienic, and less simple to service.

After a third patent of 1872, which embodied his principal improvements, Hiram Codd entered into agreements with the glassmaker, Ben Rylands, of the Hope Glass Works, Barnsley, Yorkshire. Many of the surviving bottles bear the name of the firm, Rylands & Codd, moulded on them in relief. After the death of Ben Rylands in 1881 bottles were marked Codd & Rylands, but Codd remained a partner for only three further years. By 1884 he found that he could not work amicably with Ryland's son, Dan, or vice versa. Both Hiram Codd and Dan Rylands continued independently to modify the bottles, but Codd died three years later at the age of fifty.

Rylands tried the device of giving the bottle-lips distinctive colours, and promising his customers that no two of them in the same area would be supplied with the same colour. It was done in an effort to prevent firms using each other's bottles, but did not prove successful. Rylands and other makers produced most of their bottles in a green-tinted glass, but a proportion were in amber and other colours.

The Codd bottles were supplied by English makers to

bottlers in Australia, New Zealand, South Africa, and elsewhere, and numbers of them have been found in those countries where they were abandoned by their users. The efficacy of the device in its later forms is amply proved by unopened examples that have stayed gas-tight since the day they were filled (Plate 11). Although Hiram Codd died in 1887, use of his bottle continued for a further half century or more. In England Olive Talbot noted that they were still being made as late as 1947.

For a few years another bottle attempted to challenge the Codd, but without success. It was what the inventor, W. J. Haynes, advertised as 'The Bottle of the Future', claiming that it was superior in many ways to Codd's. Its main difference was that in place of a spherical marble in the neck, it had one of cylindrical shape with rounded ends. Haynes considered that this would be of no interest to young vandals, as it would have been useless in a game of marbles: the object of acquiring the prize in the neck of a Codd bottle.

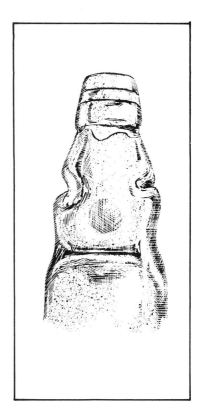

A flat-based Hamilton bottle supplanted the earlier egg shape, but the date of its introduction is as yet uncertain. It was easier to fill, could stand upright, and with the introduction of the Crown cork it gained an extended lease of life. The Crown cork was a cork-lined crimped metal closure that gripped a shallow rim moulded on the outside of the neck of the bottle. It was removable with a special tool that was cheap and simple, but once off the Crown stayed off and was not re-usable. It was invented by a Baltimore man, William Painter, and patented in 1892.

Slightly earlier, two other closures had been introduced: the internal screw and the swing stopper. The latter had a glass or vulcanized-rubber stopper with a rubber seal and was designed to swing into and out of position by means of a linked wire hinge. The internal screw type was made of wood or vulcanite, again with a rubber washer, and screwed into a thread moulded for it within the neck of the bottle. It was patented in 1879 by Henry Barrett.

In America the Hutchinson stopper, a rubber plug with a strong wire going through it leaving a loop at the top, was widely adopted. The plug was pulled up inside the neck of the bottle where it was held in place by friction and gas pressure, being released by hitting the projecting loop. 'Hutchinson's Patent Spring Soda Bottle Stopper' was devised by Charles G. Hutchinson of Chicago and patented in 1879. It was in use until the close of the cen-

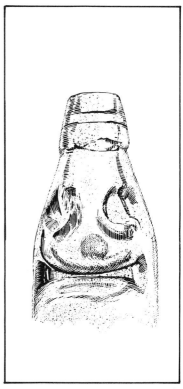

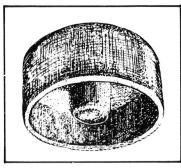

Turned wood Codd-bottle opener; the glass marble was pushed down by the peg protruding inside the opener

Crown cork of crimped metal with a cork liner, patented by William Painter of Baltimore, Maryland, in 1892

tury, when the Crown cork supplanted it. The latter completely covered the top edge of the bottle so that it was more hygienic, and it enjoyed a long-lived international success.

Typical of a number of competing American aerated drinks is Coca Cola, first made at Atlanta, Georgia, in the mid 1880s. From about 1894 it was marketed in bottles with Hutchinson stoppers, and a few years later most bottlers of it had transferred to the Crown cork. The still-familiar 'hobble-skirt' pattern of bottle was adopted as standard in 1915.

During the years from about 1870 onwards there were innumerable patents granted in many countries for all kinds of ingenious bottles and closures. Many of them failed to be adopted because too much financial risk was involved in making special bottles for particular closures; others were, like 'Haynes's 'Bottle of the Future', in the words of Olive Talbot, 'born out of . . . time, invented too late'. Others again demanded costly apparatus in the form of special machines to fill them. It can be seen that those few ingenious men who were able to overcome all the obstacles and objections finally to achieve success fully deserved it.

Swing stopper, one of
several of the type patented in
the late 1870s

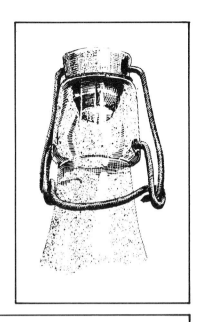

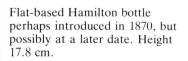

Flat-based Hamilton bottle
perhaps introduced in 1870, but
possibly at a later date. Height
17.8 cm.

Bottle-neck with internal
thread for a wood screw stopper,
introduced c. 1880

'Hutchinson's Patent
Spring Soda Bottle Stopper',
patented by Charles G.
Hutchinson, of Chicago, in 1879

Perfume Bottles

Perfumes were probably sold in phials of the kinds used by apothecaries. The most popular of all perfumes, eau de Cologne, was certainly first supplied in phial-type flasks known as *Rosolenflaschen* (Plate 33). This strong connexion between a perfume and a medicine existed because the scented water was then sold as a panacea.

Eau de Cologne was successfully marketed early in the eighteenth century by Johann Maria Farina, an Italian who had emigrated to Cologne. With each *Rosolenflasche* the purchaser was given a printed sheet listing the ailments for which it provided relief or a cure, and instructions for taking it. Translated by Edmund Launert, the sheet of paper reads, in part, that the contents of the phial should be taken

> once or twice a week in a dose of fifty to sixty drops in wine, water, warm broth, or other liquids, as a remedy against stomach upsets, headaches, toothache, unrequited love, labour pains, halitosis, strokes or even as a prophylactic against the plague.

Farina was succeeded in business by his nephew, but the firm continuously attracted rivals. Many of them adopted the forenames and surname of the original, so that at the Great Exhibition of 1851 there were four separate displays mounted by 'Johann Maria Farina', all of them with different addresses in Cologne. It was remarked at the time that 'speculation is carried to so high a pitch in Cologne, that any child, entitled to the surname of Farina is bargained for as soon as born, and christened Johann Maria; at times this event is even anticipated'.

One of the four Farinas showing at the Exhibition used the device of a small fountain playing eau de Cologne, which intrigued the public and gained the exhibitor an honourable mention from the jury granting awards. Two of his namesakes earned the same, and the fourth achieved the distinction of a prize medal.

American coloured and clear flat-sided bottles, variously shaped and moulded with patterns, were allegedly used for containing toilet preparations. Irrespective of the possibility that many of them were otherwise employed, they are usually referred to as 'perfume bottles' (Plate 34). The earliest of them bear such patterns as the 'diamond daisy', a formal flower within a diamond-shaped border, or simple fluting and lozenges, and all were made in amethyst and other colours. They are attributed to the Stiegel glassworks in Pennsylvania and date from about 1780. Nineteenth-century bottles apparently used for the same purpose vary widely in design, some of them resembling the contemporary spirit flasks, moulded with scrolls, sunbursts, and other patterns. A few depicted, appropriately, bunches of flowers, others took the form of standing Orientals, stoppered through their turbanned heads, or seated bears with removable heads; these last were used for Bear's Grease, a popular hair dressing.

The Beilby and Bewick workshop engraved moulds for one concern that was unarguably connected with the sale of perfume. In 1819 they repaired a mould for the firm of Price and Gosnell, and in the following year lettered three moulds with the inscription 'Price and Gosnell Perfumers to His Majesty' in 'small letters' at 3d. a letter. Further orders followed until 1829, when they cut 'Price and Gosnell 160 Regent Street'. 'Atkinson London', engraved in 1817, could well have been for James Atkinson, wholesale perfumer, of 44 Gerrard Street, London, but there is no certainty that the mould was for his products.

Flask moulded with a sailing ship. American, mid-19th century, height 12 cm.

Clear and matt glass
perfume bottle. Probably French,
early 20th century, height 12 cm.

Olive-green flask moulded
with a sunburst design. American,
perhaps New Hampshire, *c.*
1820, height 18.4 cm.

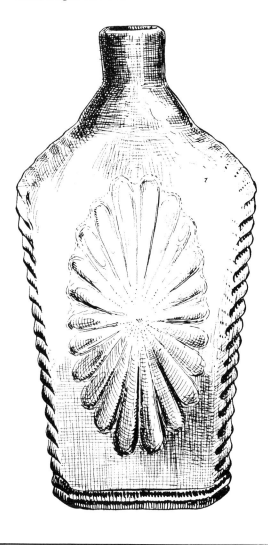

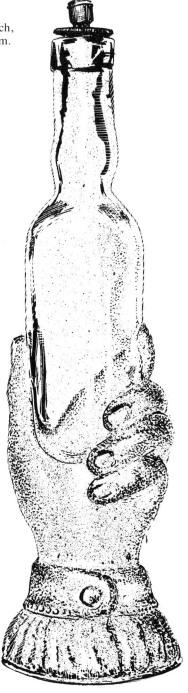

Pharmacy Bottles

Small-sized Roman glass bottles or phials dating from the first century A.D. onwards have been found in tombs in many parts of the world. Many of them are pear-shaped or bulbous in outline, and are frequently referred to as 'tear bottles', either in reference to their shape or because it has been thought, erroneously, that they had been used to preserve the tears of the dead or of weeping mourners.

The Roman phials were blown thinly of a green-tinted metal, as were later pharmacy bottles made in England. There are, however, differences in finish and often differences in shape: the more usual English form being straight-sided with a short neck and out-turned rim, and the distinguishing feature of a pronounced kick-up. Phials of the type were in use from about the sixteenth century until nearly 1800 (Plate 32). Early in the seventeenth century many such containers were octagonal in section, and occasionally more complex shapes appeared in the 1750s.

The best known of the latter was the cello-shaped bottle used by Robert Turlington for his 'Remedy for Every Malady', Turlington's Balsam of Life. The potion was patented in 1744, and one of his bottles, dated in relief 26 March 1750, has been recovered from an old well at Colonial Williamsburg.

Turlington's bottle was of clear glass, although others were made of green metal. The surviving account for glassware supplied to Guy's Hospital, London, reprinted by J. K. Crellin and J. R. Scott, includes vessels in both green and flint glass. Daniel Defoe provides further confirmation of the practice at the time; in his *Complete English Tradesman* of 1727 he noted that several glasshouses included in their output 'fine flint glass' phials for chemists and apothecaries. In the following year the Dennis glasshouse at Stourbridge could supply 'flint viols at three Shillings and sixpence for one Hundred and fifty in number. Green Viols at two shillings for one hundred and fifty'.

Prices of phials in the seventeenth century have only occasionally been recorded, their value being about $\frac{1}{2}$d. apiece with larger ones at $\frac{3}{4}$d. In 1632 an Oxfordshire mercer had in his assorted stock '20 viales glasses at 10d. a doz.' Later, in 1696, in the same county, George Ecton or Acton of Abingdon, who was termed 'potter' but probably only retailed pottery along with glass and much else, had in stock:

> 2 grooce ½ of viall glasses at 5s. [a gross]
> 7 dos. of large vialls at 9d. [a dozen]

These are, however, extracts from a probate inventory and retail prices were higher.

While glass remained untaxed, between 1699 and 1745, lead glass would probably have been used for making many phials, the alternative description of it as 'flint' being current at the time. The habit of using a clear glass for such articles persisted after 1745, but it seems that the highly-taxed flint metal was replaced by a cheaper potash glass decolourized with arsenic and manganese.

In 1758, and again in 1764, Robert Dossie included a recipe for 'Best Phial Glass' in his book *The Handmaid to the Arts*. It contained white sand, potash, common salt, arsenic, and a small amount of manganese. Dossie commented;

> This will be a very good glass for the purpose; and will work with a moderate heat: but requires time to become clear, on account of the proportion of arsenic: when, however, it is once in good condition, it will come very near to the chrystal-glass.

The practice of using a non-lead glass that was liable to a lower rate of duty was doubtless noticed and frowned upon by the authorities, who were always interested in increasing revenue. In 1777 the Excise duties were raised: bottle glass to be charged at 3s. 6d. per 112 lb., and flint at 18s. 8d., and at the same time the opportunity was taken to include 'all phial glass, commonly called or known by the name of apothecary or other phials' in the last category. A phial was defined as having a capacity of 6 fluid ounces (22·73ml.) or less, and bottle-makers did not go below that limit. In fact, the Act of 1811 laid down that they should not make 'any bottles of less size and content than what is commonly deemed and reputed a half-pint bottle'. The actual position was explained to the 1835 Commissioners by Richard Shortridge, of Newcastle upon Tyne, who said:

> The law says, the reputed half-pint, which should be eight ounces; but under some quibble in the wording of the Act, or from the connivance of the officers, they make them six ounces.

Among other glassmakers who gave evidence before the Commissioners was Apsley Pellatt, of London, who had formerly been a manufacturer but by that date was confining his activities to retailing the ware. In response to a question about the goods made legally and holding under a half-pint, he replied:

> An immense amount of six and eight ounce medicine bottles, oval, octagon, and square, are made by bottle glass manufacturers; also green round six ounce phials.

Asked whether makers were prohibited from producing phials of black glass, William Powell, a Bristol glass-maker, answered:

> Yes, or even calling them phials; we make bottles the same shape, six and eight ounces, but we call them by a different name; we are not allowed to make under six ounces in black glass.

In 1824 flint and phial glass paid duty at the rate of £4. 18s. per 112 lb., and bottle glass at 8s. 2d. In the following year a change took place in the method of collection and the duty on flint and phial glass was levied by weight. The fluxed materials were charged 3d. per pound, plus 6d. per pound 'on the excess of the weight of the manufactured article above the weight of the material'. Soon afterwards, in 1828, the duty on bottle glass was reduced to 7s. per 112lb., but on flint and phial glass it remained unaltered. The throttling tangle of continually changing rules and rates, their interpretation and evasion, was finally swept away when the duties were abolished in 1845. Clear or coloured or black bottles were then to be obtained in any size, and the sick were no longer penalized by what had been, in effect, a tax on curative medicine.

Supplying of medicines in bottles holding a dozen or so doses began to take place early in the nineteenth century, but it was not until the close of Victoria's reign that the familiar flat, rectangular bottle appeared. Doses were at first marked on a printed slip pasted to the back of the bottle, but before long they were moulded in relief on the bottle itself.

Carelessness and ignorance in taking medicines so often led to accidental poisoning and death, that in the mid nineteenth century attention was directed to lessening the risks. Then, and in the decades following, bottles were specially designed to give clear warning to whoever handled them. Bright green or bright blue glass was employed, and this was moulded with ribs, flutes, or bosses, so that a message was conveyed instantly by touch or sight. Inventive ingenuity in this direction was not limited to Europe, and in America a stopper bristling with tiny sharp points was devised. In that country, too, a patent was granted in 1890 for a bottle in the shape of a coffin with a skull and crossbones and 'POISON' on the front. In the same vein was a bottle moulded as a skull with the neck of the container rising from the apex and the word 'POISON' in relief on the forehead; an unmistakeable, if macabre, way of conveying a warning (Plate 00).

The Beilby and Bewick workshop papers, transcribed by Margaret Ellison, throw light on many of the moulded and relief-lettered bottles produced in the Newcastle area in the early nineteenth century. The brief details record the wording required, by which mould-maker the order was given, the name of the bottle-maker concerned, the date of ordering, and the cost.

Among the most consistent users were the makers of Daffy's Elixir, a long-lived panacea first marketed in the seventeenth century, mentioned by Dickens in *Oliver Twist,* and still available in the early decades of the present century. Moulds, lettered either 'Daffy's Elixir' or 'True Daffy's Elixir' were ordered between 1786 and 1825, and in one instance, in 1822, a pewter mould was used, cut with 90 letters at a cost of 15s. For a comparable remedy, Turlington's Balsam, which has already been mentioned, a mould was cut in 1816; 76 letters for £1 17s. 6d. or 6d. a letter, which was the average price. In the following year another was executed, on this occasion with 86 letters. The shape of the bottles is not specified, so it is unknown whether they were of the 'cello' outline formerly used, but it is recorded that they were made by Shortridge & Co., of South Shields.

Other preparations sold in moulded and lettered bottles made in the Newcastle area (the date of ordering added in brackets) included: Dalby's Carminative (1815 and 1816), Fens Embrocation (1803), Fosters Rheumatic Drops (1805 and 1806), Lowe's Balsam (1823), Masons Carminative Cordial (1818), Sibly's Solar Tincture (1815), Smiths Penetrating Application (1821), and the hair-oil that gave its name to the upholstery protector, the anti-Macassar, Rowlands Macassar Oil (1811). Of the foregoing, two moulds were cut in 1815 for Sibly's Solar Tincture, the bottles being supplied by Shortridge & Co., and the Northumberland Glass Co.

Sometimes moulds were sent to the workshop for re-cutting or repair, probably because they had become worn in use. Thus, in 1815 an order was taken to 'repair and deepen mould' lettered 'C. Ramsay Penrith Cumberland Bituminous Fluid', in 1821 to 'repair mould' of 'Ramsay's Pastoral [?Pectoral] Balsam', and the same year to recut 'Ramsay 74 @ 2d'. The last-named suggesting a further lease of life being given to the Bituminous Fluid that had been noted in 1815 as also having 74 letters.

There are instances of surgeons and chemists having named bottles to contain medicines they dispensed; they served as advertisements or possibly to remind users to return the vessels when emptied. The rare surviving examples are sealed and date from the early 1800s. W. Williams of Llandovery, Carmarthenshire, adding his profession of surgeon, but S. Jewel only giving his initial and surname. Local knowledge supplied the information that members of the Jewel family had been surgeons at St. Columb, Cornwall.

Newcastle glasshouses supplied moulded bottles for the same purpose, and the Beilby and Bewick workshop cut the lettering on the moulds. Among others were the undermentioned, with the date of ordering in brackets: 'Prepared by W. Davison Chemist etc. 34 [letters] @ 4d.' (1817); 'T. Jollie Druggist Dundee' (1810); 'Lockwood Chemist York' (1824); 'Marshall Apothecary High Street Berwick' (1825); and 'Martindale Chemist etc.' (1823). In addition, bottles with seals lettered 'Gibett Surgeon' were supplied by Isaac Cookson & Son of Newcastle in 1802.

From early in the 1800s it would appear that a moulded and lettered bottle was preferred to a sealed one, not improbably because the former would have been cheaper. A further reason can be found in the great increase in population that took place between 1801 and 1831; between those years the number of inhabitants of Great Britain rose dramatically from eleven million to sixteen and a half million. The demand for all kinds of goods likewise increased, and the old-style craftsman began to find that his best speed was insufficient under the circumstances. The carefully-placed, stamped seal took too much time in the making; the mould provided an adequate, if less pleasing, substitute.

The premises of the chemist or apothecary required a number of bottles in which to store the ingredients of medicines, whether in solid, powder, or liquid form. Those standing overall 15–30cm. in height were known as Shop Rounds. It was usual for the labels on the Rounds to receive attention, so that the inscription naming the contents was decorative as well as informative. In the majority of instances the lettering was in black on a gilt ground, but occasionally it was engraved in the glass within a border of flourishes.

In the second half of the nineteenth century the bottles were often made with a rectangular recess in the side, and into this was cemented a curved glass lettered on the inside. Such bottles were made on both sides of the Atlantic. A patent was granted in America in 1862 to W. N. Walton and renewed five years later, while in England bottles with the mark of the York Glass Company bear similar designations termed at the time 'patent phototype labels'. The Yorkshire firm's mark is found in relief beneath the base: 'Y G Co.' inside a hexagon.

The Shop Rounds were not always of clear glass, among the attractive colours in which they exist is an opaque pale blue. As occurred with medicine bottles, those intended for poisons were often made in blue or green glass, ribbed or otherwise moulded and often hexagonal in shape (Plate 17). While the Rounds for dry drugs had close-fitting stoppers, those for syrups were not ground-in but had plug-ends that rested loosely inside the short neck so that they did not stick. Some bottles had restricted necks so that the liquid in them could be poured out drop by drop.

The Newcastle records show that a number of moulds were cut with inscriptions apposite to both medicine and shop bottles. Available evidence in two instances points to the latter: in 1813 the wording 'Tyne Dispensary' was charged 10s 6d. or 9d. a letter, compared with 6d. a letter noted for medicine bottles. Further the entry states 'large mould', as does that for 'Boston Dispensary' (1806). In other instances there can be less certainty: 'Lynn Dispensary' was cut in February 1813 for 10s. 6d. (9d. a letter) but in October of the same year and in 1816 for 7s. (6d. a letter), which suggests that both sizes of bottles were supplied. Among other institutions concerned were 'Alnwick Dispensary' (1826), 'Jedburgh Dispensary' (1829), 'Newcastle Infirmary' (1824), 'Plymouth Hospitals' (1800), and 'Haslar' (1800). The last-named being the Royal Hospital for Seamen at Haslar, Gosport, built between 1751 and 1762. 'Manchester Infirm^y' was cut on a seal in 1816.

Use of display bottles by chemists was not confined to the shop interior: the street-window of the premises nor-

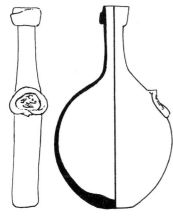

Riga Balsam bottle. 19th century, height 12.6 cm.

mally received no less attention. Pride of place was given to a set of show globes, often three in number, filled with coloured liquids that looked equally attractive in daylight or artificial light. In time, the handsome globes became accepted as the sign of a chemist, in the same way as a carved wood figure of a Highlander with his mull proclaimed a tobacconist. As early as 1778 William Drewet Smith of Burling-Slip, New York, advertised in the *Royal Gazette* that he had in stock 'nests of drawers, show glasses &c.'

Sets of square-section stoppered bottles were supplied in portable brass-bound mahogany chests for the use of travellers and for home use. The bottles were in sizes according to the likely amount of contents required, and usually had printed labels on them (Plate 16). Those lettered 'Brandy' are invariably now empty.

Seal

Green glass Riga Balsam bottle. 19th century, height 11.2 cm.

One bottled medicinal preparation has been the subject of argument. Riga Balsam was employed mainly as a carminative, a type of medicine described by the sixteenth-century writer John Florio as one that made 'grose humours fine and thin', or in modern parlance a reliever of flatulence. Some energetic salesmen stressed its more extensive curative properties, and an American advertised his beliefs in the pages of a Savannah newspaper of 1801. He suggested that buyers might test the product in a way that would resolve any doubts of its efficacy:

> Take a hen, drive a nail through it's scull, brains and [t]ongue, then pour some of it [the Balsam] into the wound it will directly stop the bleeding, cure it in 8 or 6 minutes, and it will eat as before.

In Europe, Riga Balsam was manufactured in Russia and exported through the Baltic seaport of Riga, (hence the name). It was sold in a pale-green glass flask with a flat-sided round body and long neck, measuring about 12cm. long overall and 7·5cm. wide, with a small seal on the shoulder that led to the argument mentioned above. The first record of the seal and its wording appeared in the correspondence columns of the *Sunday Times* in the late 1940s, because a bottle of the type, in the Yorkshire Museum, York, had had the lettering on its seal read as 'PIG BAG'. Under this title and with inconclusive comment it was included by Lady Sheelah Ruggles-Brise in her book *Sealed Bottles,* because letters in the newspaper, initiated by her inquiry, had produced no satisfactory answer.

There the matter rested until 1976, when visitors to the exhibition of bottles at the County Museum, Truro, saw both the Yorkshire bottle and another almost identical to it. The latter matched the other in colour and shape, but the seal was clearly worded 'RIGA BALSAM'. The Pharmaceutical Society of Great Britain drew attention to an article in a Dutch journal by Dr. D. A. Wittop Koning, in which a labelled and sealed bottle was illustrated. The unusual shape of the original bottle, the fact that it bore a seal, and the poor quality of the metal all led to a supposition that it was older than it looked. Despite their appearance, it is probable that the two discussed, and other matching bottles, date to sometime in the nineteenth century; this being the case whether they are sealed in English with the words 'RIGA BALSAM', or in Latin with '*Riga Balsem Olie*'.

Preserves Bottles

Bottles with bodies closely resembling those of normal wine bottles but with much wider necks and mouths were made from the late seventeenth/early eighteenth century. Their precise purpose cannot be determined, but it is probable that they were used for holding preserves of many kinds. William Salmon in his *Family Dictionary* of 1705 gives numerous recipes for pickles and preserved fruits. Cherries are to be boiled in syrup, then 'put them into glasses, and cover them two or three days later'. After scalding mushrooms in herb-flavoured water, 'put them afterwards into glasses that they may be very closely stopt . . . and so close them up with a Cover of Leather for your use' (Plate 9).

Contemporary mentions of the containers are infrequent. One appeared in the pages of the *Boston Gazette* of 28 July 1760. Jonathan Williams, 'near the Swing Bridge', advertised for sale 'half Gallon and Gallon wide-mouth'd Pickle Bottles'. Another was in the *New-York Gazette,* 8 February 1773, where there was a notice of goods 'Removed from the store kept by Mr. Henry Wm. Stiegel, near the Exchange, to the store of James and Arthur Jarvis, between Burling and Beekman's Slips, in the Fly'. The articles offered included all kinds of glass for the table, and 'wide-mouth bottles for sweetmeats'.

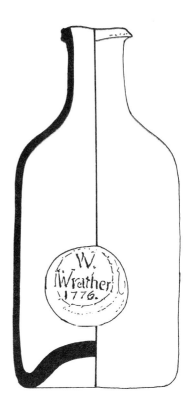

Wide-mouthed bottle sealed W. Wrathe[n] 1776. Height 22.1 cm.

Serving Bottles

A serving bottle, or decanter bottle, is a wine bottle made with a handle to one side. Such bottles are assumed to have been used at the table, and are a stage in the development of the decanter. A sealed pale-green example in the Victoria and Albert Museum, London, is dated 1717, and a few others of black glass bear dates between about 1700 and 1725. A nineteenth-century handled flagon in pale-green glass, sealed 'W Trease 1821', appears to be unique, but there may be similar ones unrecorded.

Spirit Flasks

The spirit flask, as has been mentioned earlier, was a product of nineteenth-century America. Many of the designs found on their sides would have been appreciated only in that land, where their political or other subtleties were an attraction to buyers. Discounting these locally-inspired features, even those with patterns of a wider appeal are seldom seen beyond the borders of the land where they were made.

The patterns used at first included spiral and horizontal ribbing, sunbursts, a cornucopia brimming with produce, and, occasionally, the American eagle. From the close of the second decade of the nineteenth century the various manufacturers adopted more ambitious designs, many of them patriotic and depicting national heroes. Others showed distinguished visitors, like Jenny Lind, who was rapturously received when she toured the country in 1851–2. Many of the designs vividly commemorate the history and customs of the period, as well as the abilities of the glassmakers of the time.

The flasks were made with capacities of a quart, pint, and half-pint, and in several colours, including green, amber, various shades of blue and amethyst, clear glass, and milk-white. They varied in silhouette over the years; for example, many of the later flasks were made with longer necks than had formerly been the case.

A number of the flasks bear the name and location of the maker, among whom the most renowned is Thomas Dyott, of the Kensington (later Dyottville) Glass Works, Philadelphia. His portrait flasks are distinguished by their clear-cut moulding, and he may perhaps be excused for including his own bust on the reverse of a flask depicting Benjamin Franklin. Less worthy was the addition to his name of the initials M.D.; he was not a doctor, but possibly considered that his competing profession of vendor of patent medicines was sufficient justification for awarding himself the qualification.

The flasks faded out of production towards the close of the century. Among the reasons for their disappearance was the disruption caused by the Civil War, the onward march of the temperance movement, and probably a diminished appeal to the public in the face of fresh novelties.

Whisky and Whiskey Bottles

In Scotland, where it is produced, whisky was supplied in plain bottles like those used for wine. The makers no doubt considered that their discerning patrons could distinguish their favourite brand from others without the aid

Olive-amber spirit flask moulded with a named portrait bust of George Washington. American, New Hampshire, *c.* 1830, height 17.2 cm.

96

of meretricious containers. In America a pseudo-Scottish liquid was given the name 'whiskey', pronounced in the same way as the genuine heather dew but with the added, silent, 'e'. There, many of the makers vied with each other in tempting the eye of the drinker as well as his palate. The best-known and most remarkable of the bottles employed for the purpose was that of E.G. Booz, of Philadelphia. It was in the shape of a cabin with door and windows, bears the date 1840, and was first marketed in the 1860s. It may be thought, perhaps, that the felicitously-named Booz gave his name to liquor and drinking, but in fact the words booze or bouse were current with those meanings in the seventeenth century.

Light green Booz's 'Old Cabin' whiskey bottle. American, New Jersey, c. 1870, height 17.8 cm.

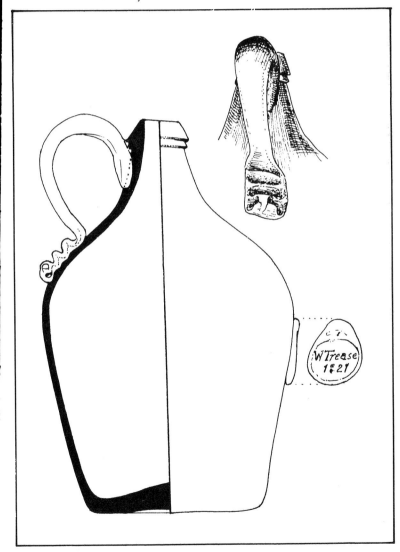

Pale green serving bottle, 1821. Height 25 cm.

A NOTE FOR BOTTLE COLLECTORS

It is true to say that anything for which there is a market has its imitations. This applies to both modern and old articles, and certainly to the ever-widening range of objects classified under the heading of 'Antiques'.

It will be found that bottles have suffered their share of attention from those eager to supply the demand for them. Resins have been found useful in affixing seals to hitherto innocently plain bottles. If some of the lettering on it is inconvenient, a moulded bottle can be transformed from the mediocre to the desirable by skilful use of grinding and polishing wheels. The mauve tint seen on pre-1915 bottles exposed to sunshine, esteemed by many, can be artificaly induced with the aid of ultra-violet and other rays.

Numerous reproductions of nineteenth-century American spirit flasks have been made, some of them differing in minor details of design from the originals, others varying from them in colour. Most of these have been minutely studied and listed with the devotion and skill of a bibliographer.

Less likely to deceive are the seals moulded on modern wine bottles. They can very occasionally mislead the inexperienced, but the complete absence of the undercutting visible where a hand-applied seal joins the bottle is a clear indication. Some nineteenth-century bottles were machine-made but hand-sealed, in which case the finish of the base of the bottle reveals the disparity in techniques.

On the whole, at the time of writing, fakes of bottles are comparatively few and seldom of a high standard. If a collector takes trouble to train his eye he will seldom, if ever, be imposed upon.

Select Bibliography

James Barrelet, *La Verrerie en France,* Paris, 1953

Francis Buckley, 'Early Glasshouses of Bristol', in *Journal of the Society of Glass Technology,* Vol. IX, Sheffield, 1925

——, 'Glasshouses on the Tyne in the 18th century', ibid., Vol. X, 1926

——, 'Old Lancashire Glasshouses', ibid. Vol. XIII, 1929

J. L. Carvel, *Alloa Glass Work,* privately published, 1953

Raymond Chambon, *L'Histoire de la verrerie en Belgique du IIme siècle à nos jours,* Brussels, 1955

J. K. Crellin and J. R. Scott, *Glass and British Pharmacy 1600–1900: a Survey and Guide to the Wellcome Collection,* 1972

[Robert Dossie], *The Handmaid to the Arts,* 2 vols., 1758

R. W. Douglas and S. Frank, *A History of Glassmaking,* 1972

George Francis Dow (Ed.), *The Arts and Crafts in New England 1704–1755,* Topsfield, Mass., 1927

G. Eland (Ed.), *Purefoy Letters 1735–1753,* 2 vols., 1931

Margaret Ellison, 'The Tyne Glasshouses and *Beilby and Bewick* Workshop', in *Archaeologia Aeliana,* 5th Series, Vol. III, Newcastle upon Tyne, 1975

Eleanor S. Godfrey, *The Development of English Glassmaking 1560–1640,* University of North Carolina Press, Chapel Hill, 1975

Ruth Susswein Gottesman (Ed.), *The Arts and Crafts in New York 1726–1776,* New York, 1938

D. R. Guttery, *From Broad Glass to Cut-Crystal,* 1956

Albert Hartshorne, *Old English Glasses,* 1897; reprinted as *Antique Drinking Glasses,* New York, 1967

Jeremy Haslam, 'Oxford Taverns and the Cellars of All Souls in the 17th and 18th centuries', in *Oxoniensia,* XXXIV, 1969, Oxford, 1970

——, 'Sealed Bottles from All Souls College', ibid. XXXV, 1970, 1971

W. B. Honey, *Glass, a Handbook,* 1946

James Howell, *Epistolae Ho-Elianae,* third edition, 1655

J. Paul Hudson, 'Seventeenth Century Glass Wine Bottles and Seals excavated at Jamestown', in *Journal of Glass Studies,* III, Corning, N.Y., 1961

Ivor Noël Hume, 'The Glass Wine Bottle in Colonial Virginia', in *Journal of Glass Studies,* III, Corning, N.Y., 1961

——, *A Guide to Artifacts of Colonial America,* New York, 1970

F. W. Hunter, *Stiegel Glass,* New York, 1914 (reprinted 1950)

Olive Jones, 'Glass Bottle Push-ups and Pontil Marks', in *Historical Archaeology,* Vol. V, Lansing, Michigan, 1971

William C. Ketchum, Jr., *A Treasury of American Bottles*, Indianapolis, 1975
D. A. Wittop Koning, 'Riga Balsem', in *Pharmaceutisch Weekblad*, 109, 1974
Edmund Launert, *Scent and Scent Bottles*, 1974
Helen McKearin, *Bottles, Flasks and Dr. Dyott*, New York, 1970
Leslie G. Matthews, *Antiques of the Pharmacy*, 1971
Edward Meigh, *The Story of the Glass Bottle*, Stoke-on-Trent, 1972
Roy Morgan, *Sealed Bottles*, Burton-on-Trent, (1976)
Cecil Munsey, *The Illustrated Guide to Collecting Bottles*, New York, 1970
W. M. Myddelton, *Chirk Castle Accounts 1666–1753*, Manchester, 1931
Emma Papert, *The Illustrated Guide to American Glass*, New York, 1972
A. C. Powell, 'Glass-Making in Bristol', in *Transactions of the Bristol and Gloucestershire Archaeological Society*, Vol. XLVII, Gloucester, 1926
Sheelah Ruggles-Brise, *Sealed Bottles*, 1949
Gerald Stevens, *Early Canadian Glass*, Toronto, 1961
Olive Talbot, 'The Evolution of Glass Bottles for Carbonated Drinks', in *Post-Medieval Archaeology*, Vol. 8, 1974
Gladys Scott Thomson, *Life in a Noble Household 1641–1700*, 1937
——, *Letters of a Grandmother 1732–1735*, 1943
——, *Family Background*, 1949
W. A. Thorpe, *A History of English and Irish Glass*, 2 vols., 1929
——, 'The Glass Sellers' Bills at Woburn Abbey', in *Journal of the Society of Glass Technology*, Vol., XXII, Sheffield, 1938
Andrew Ure, *A Dictionary of Arts, Manufactures, and Mines*, 2 vols., 1853
D. G. Vaisey and F. S. C. Celoria, 'Inventory of George Ecton, Potter, of Abingdon, Berks., 1696', in *Journal of Ceramic History*, No. 7, Stafford, 1974
John Wade, 'Some Early Australian Glass', in *Australasian Antique Collector*, XVII, 1976
Geoffrey Wills, *English and Irish Glass*, 1968
——, *English Glass Bottles for the Collector*, 1974
Victor Wyatt, *From Sand-core to Automation*, revised edition, 1972
James Harvey Young, *The Toadstool Millionaires: a Social History of Patent Medicines in America before Federal Times*, Princeton, N.J., 1961
Thirteenth Report of the Commissioners of Inquiry into the Excise Establishment . . . Glass, 1835
Wine Trade Loan Exhibition Catalogue, 1933
The Compleat Imbiber, catalogue of an exhibition commemorating the centenary of W. & A. Gilbey, Ltd., 1957
The English Glass Bottle through the Ages, catalogue of an exhibition held at The County Museum, Truro, Cornwall, 1976

Index

Numerals in bold type refer to the colour plates.

102

The colour photographs are reproduced with the kind permision of the undermentioned :